# Audubon®

## POCKET BACKYARD BIRDWATCH

# LONDON, NEW YORK, MUNICH, MELBOURNE, DELHI

**Project Editor** Rebecca Warren
**Project Art Editor** Francis Wong
**Editorial Assistant** Lizzie Munsey
**Design Assistant** Riccie Janus
**Production Editor** Vania Cuhna
**Production** Shane Higgins
**Managing Editor** Sarah Larter
**Managing Art Editor** Phil Ormerod
**Publisher** Jonathan Metcalf
**Art Director** Bryn Walls

First American edition 2008 published in the
United States by DK Publishing
345 Hudson Street, New York, New York 10014

The revised edition published in the United
States in 2010 by DK Publishing

11 12 13 14  10 9 8 7 6 5 4
004–176110–Feb/02

Copyright © 2007, 2010 Dorling Kindersley Ltd.
All rights reserved

A CIP catalog record for this book is available
from the Library of Congress

ISBN  978-0-7566-5864-9

Color reproduction by Media Development
Printing Ltd. in the UK

Printed and bound in China by LEO Paper
Products Ltd.

Discover more at
**www.dk.com**

# Contents

# Introduction

**Owners of backyards large and small can help birds. The need for backyard sanctuary has never been more urgent: each year over two million acres of undeveloped countryside in the US is lost to suburban housing with barren lawns— even the most common birds need our help.**

## Attracting birds

Birds add much to our enjoyment of the outdoors with their bright colors and beautiful songs. As stewards of all wildlife, people can help birds thrive by meeting their basic requirements: food, water, shelter, and nesting places. If you meet their needs, both resident and migratory birds will favor your property and you will benefit from their songs and antics throughout the year as different species come and go. Birds are also garden helpers that readily glean garden pests for themselves and their young.

**Garden oasis**
*Providing a source of water will reward you with close-up views of many different birds, such as these House Sparrows, bathing and drinking.*

## Using this book

This pocket guide includes sections on bird behavior, attracting birds, and tips on bird identification. The chapter on bird biology and behavior is intended to demonstrate some of the remarkable ways that birds survive, sensing the world with vision and hearing that we can only begin to imagine. Their ability to migrate, find mates, and raise

**Bird feeders**
*Provide the right foods and American Goldfinches will flock to your feeders. But food is only one of their basic requirements. Also provide water, cover, and nesting places.*

young, all while eluding predators, gives ample reason to view birds with complete awe.

The chapter on attracting birds to your backyard not only provides plans for houses and feeders but also offers tips on planting bird-friendly trees and shrubs to mimic natural habitats, and maintaining feeders and houses in order to make them safe for birds. Finally, the chapter on bird identification offers tips for recognizing birds so that you can participate in the Great Backyard Bird Count and eBird—two of the new generation of Internet-based programs that make every birding trip an opportunity to further bird conservation at the same time as you hone your own skills.

## Attracting birds

Properties of any size can provide improved habitats for birds. The essential approach is to mimic natural habitats by arranging plants in a manner similar to the way they occur in nature. For properties with well-established trees, shrubs, and vines, it is important to inventory the existing plants in your backyard and to supplement these with additional choices. For properties with few plants, there are many opportunities to establish plant communities that are especially valuable for birds. This amounts to selecting native species that are adapted for your local climate, soil, and light exposure.

Plants provide food, shelter, nesting places, and singing perches, but some species can be attracted closer with supplemental foods such as sunflower and suet. Since tree cavities are usually scarce, many species are limited by the number of available nesting places, and, therefore, nest boxes are key to the survival of these species. Likewise, the amount of water can also limit the presence of birds.

## A caring community

By turning your garden into a safe haven for wild birds, you are joining a growing community who not only enjoy having birds as close neighbors, but also recognize the value of helping birds and other wildlife survive into the future. As a "bird gardener" you can document your success by participating in the Great Backyard Bird Count, a joint program of the National Audubon Society and the Cornell Laboratory of Ornithology. Each year about 90,000 people participate in this winter count.

**Colorful migrant**
*Rose-breasted Grosbeaks are seasonal visitors to birdfeeders in the East. Only adult males have the gaudy breast color.*

**Hedge bird**
*Song Sparrows (right) require brush fields or farm borders, but will also live in suburban neighborhoods near hedges and lawns with tall grass.*

**Record keeping**
*Have a notebook handy, so that you can keep a count of the number of birds visiting your garden, record interesting behavior, or even make sketches. You could even keep a garden bird diary to record events throughout the year.*

**Close-up view**
*A pair of binoculars will show your garden birds in even greater detail and provide close-up views of their behavior.*

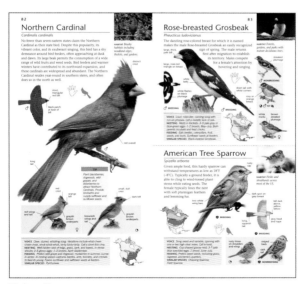

**Bird profiles**
*These detailed profiles illustrate 40 regular garden visitors. Each entry gives key information about the bird's characteristics and is illustrated by photographs of the species in the wild.*

## About birds

Birds lead remarkable, fast-paced lives.
Keep watching birds after you identify them
and read on to learn more about their family
lives and astounding migrations.

# Territory

**Varying in size from the immediate nest to several acres or more, nesting territories contain ample food, cover, and water to sustain a nesting pair and their family. Many migratory species have territories in both the nesting and wintering habitats.**

## Choosing a home

In the spring, migratory birds race back to claim their nesting territories. The first birds to arrive usually claim the best habitat, but if they arrive too early, they run the risk of extreme weather and possible starvation. This is especially true for birds such as warblers and flycatchers that feed on flying insects. Late snows are a special risk to ground-feeding birds such as robins and flickers, but these species can usually switch to fruit when necessary. Other species,

**Birdbath squabble**
*American Robins squabble over bathing space at a backyard birdbath. Birds from adjacent territories often share valuable resources such as feeders and birdbaths— but tensions can sometimes erupt during the nesting season.*

such as Pine Siskins and crossbills, nest where they find food and migrate only during years when cone-bearing trees such as pine and spruce offer little food.

## Territory defense

Male songbirds do most of the territorial defense. They typically accomplish this by maintaining a route of singing posts from which they proclaim their territory and watch for intruders. Usually song is enough to discourage neighbors from making overlapping claims, but sometimes males chase each other to enforce the boundaries. In some species, such as orioles and cardinals, females also help defend the borders by singing.

**Persistant songster**
*Male Northern Yellowthroats have a powerful song that ripples through dense, brushy tangles and hedges.*

## Winter territories

Long-distance migrants such as warblers and vireos typically set up a winter home territory that they return to year after year, and they defend this space from intruders of the same species just as they defend their nesting territory during the spring and summer. Nonmigrants such as chickadees usually group together during winter—especially in northern climates. These winter flocks consist of several breeding pairs and their young. Together, they can more effectively spot predators by day, and share their body warmth by huddling together in tree cavities at night. Other nonmigrant birds have territories but they are smaller because young birds compete for space with the adults.

**Short-distance migrant**
*Northern Flickers that nest in the northern parts of the species' range spend their winter far enough south to avoid snow, then return in early spring.*

# Singing

**Birdsong is one of the most delightful reasons for attracting birds to your garden. But what does this song mean? Typically, males produce the most elaborate and beautiful songs, while females are limited in their vocal repertoire to calls that communicate location, distress, and other messages, all unrelated to reproduction.**

## Why birds sing

Birdsong is a noncombative way for male birds to proclaim their territory and deflect intruders without risking injury by fighting. But birdsong also serves a less obvious role. Female birds assess the quality of prospective mates by selecting males that are more accomplished singers. Older birds typically have more complex songs—a trait that females admire. Older birds are also better survivors, have demonstrated immune systems, and the skill to avoid predation and find food— all qualities that females recognize as a measure of longevity, vigor, and health.

## Seasons and timing

Birdsong is most abundant in early spring as newly arriving males establish nesting territories. When nestlings hatch, the males typically help feed the young and have less time for singing. Birdsong is also more intense in the morning. In spring, the burst of song at first light is called the "dawn chorus." Birds

**Perfecting his song**
*With time and practice, male Eastern Towhees learn their species' classic song that sounds like the phrase "drink your tea." Young towhees have a more variable song than adult males.*

## SINGING PERCHES

Most songbirds sing from high perches. This permits their song to carry long distances. A shortage of "singing posts" can prevent birds from establishing a territory. Dead trees and dead branches on living trees are favorite singing posts. Thoughtful bird gardeners leave a supply of such perches for birds and are rewarded by more song.

**Fencepost songster**
*Meadowlarks often sing from fenceposts. This deters rivals from entering the territory.*

**Treetop perch**
*Like many treetop singers, Northern Parula Warblers have high-pitched, buzzy songs that carry well over the forest canopy.*

sing the most at this hour because they are reestablishing their nesting territories after they have been quiet at night.

## Recognizing bird songs

Accomplished birders can recognize most species by their songs. Some can even recognize birds by their calls—chips and chirps given by birds during the nonbreeding season. Learning to recognize birds by their voice requires practice—in much the same way that people learn to recognize each other over the telephone. To learn bird songs, try to see the bird singing—this usually involves tracking down an unusual song by moving toward or circling the sound.

**Dawn and dusk choruses**
*Eastern Bluebirds and other thrushes are known for their melodic songs, regularly performed at dawn and dusk. This reminds birds of the same species in adjacent territories that the songster is present and ready for a chase if necessary.*

# Courtship

**Female birds use the male's song and plumage to assess the quality of potential mates. Males often sport elaborate plumage and show it off in dramatic displays. Typically, birds with the best camouflaged plumage make up for their dull looks with dramatic displays and the most vibrant songs.**

## Courtship displays

Most male birds go to great lengths to attract a mate, adorning themselves with gaudy feathers and then strutting, fluffing, and otherwise displaying their colors to impress females. Wild Turkeys fan their copper-tipped tails like peacocks, and woodcocks fly more than 100 feet (30 m) above the ground to impress prospective mates. Although courtship can attract the attention of hawks and other predators, this risk is balanced against the need to attract and retain a mate.

**Courtship gift**
*Male Northern Cardinals often present their mate with food as part of their courtship. This symbolic food gesture indicates the male's potential as a provider for the future family.*

## Choosing a partner

Some pairs keep the same mate for many consecutive years—or even for a lifetime. Most, however, find a new mate each year. Those that retain the same mate

**Mate selection**
*Courtship helps insure that birds select a mate of the same species. Each species has its own unique displays. Combined with song, timing, and plumage, birds usually find a mate of the same species.*

from one year to the next typically have a shorter courtship prior to nesting, while those that must find a new mate each year spend more time and energy courting. In some species, such as woodcocks and hummingbirds, the males will attract and mate with many females. Females may also mate with neighboring males, even after choosing a partner, which increases the genetic variability in her brood.

In general, female birds select older males because they have demonstrated their ability to survive by finding ample food. Older mates are also able to avoid predators and perform successful migrations.

## Courtship behaviors

When landbirds find mates, they sometimes offer them a morsel of food. Male Northern Cardinals, for example, offer food to females, who assume a begging posture and make sounds like a nestling. This ritual helps the female decide which males will likely be able to find food for their young. Mated pairs often preen each other's neck feathers as a courtship behavior that helps synchronize the nesting pairs.

# Nesting and rearing

The nesting season begins as the days become longer. Sunlight stimulates the hormones that regulate breeding and nesting behavior. These hormones also trigger defense of the territory, song, and migration.

## The nesting season

Nesting commences when the male sets up his summer territory. For migratory species, males typically arrive first and females follow a few days or a week later. After some initial courtship, the males start singing and posturing themselves in conspicuous places. Females learn to recognize their prospective mates, which typically keep singing while the female selects the nest site and builds the nest. But there are exceptions. For example, in most wrens the male builds several nests that the female inspects and she adds the nest lining.

Birds build nests and raise young during the summer because the days are longer, offering them more light to capture their prey. There is also abundant cover to shelter nests and a great flush of insect protein—necessary for young

**Early-nesting bird**
*American Robins are early nesters and this species often builds its nest in the fork of a tree.*

birds to put on body weight while growing thousands of feathers.

## Nest construction

Bird nests represent remarkable architecture, especially considering that birds do not have hands. Instead, they use their bills and feet to collect materials and weave them into a nest. Birds use a vast array of materials including grass, sticks, bark, moss, lichen, feathers, snakeskin, hair, and even spider webs. Using their bill and feet, they masterfully weave their materials together in an instinctive manner. Birders can assist nest building by providing short sections of string or yarn (about 4 in/10 cm long), wool, dried grass, lint from dryers, and feathers. Put these materials in a hanging basket on a clothesline, or toss the feathers to the wind to watch swallows collect them.

**Cliff Swallow nest**
*Mouthfuls of mud are the primary ingredient, typically placed under a building's eves.*

**Hummingbird nest**
*The size of a half-dollar coin, these tiny nests are typically built on top of a forked tree branch.*

**Oriole nest**
*These well-woven, bag-shaped nests are hung from a tall tree, often over water or a highway.*

## Eggs and incubation

Soon after the nest is built, females begin laying eggs. Usually, songbirds lay one egg each day until the clutch is complete. Most small birds lay about four eggs, but hummingbirds typically lay two, while tiny kinglets usually lay 8–9 eggs in two layers. Eggs of birds that build open, cup-shaped nests usually have camouflaged markings, such as speckles and lines, to make them less conspicuous to predators, while those that nest in tree cavities typically have white eggs without markings. Most small birds wait until they have laid their complete clutch before they start incubation. This timing has chicks hatching at the same time so that there is less competition for food.

For species in which the sexes look similar, such as flycatchers and vireos, both sexes share incubation.

**Nest repairs**
*Most landbirds build new nests each year. This helps reduce their exposure to overwintering nest parasites.*

For those that look very different, such as tanagers, buntings, and Red-winged Blackbirds, the female does all of the incubating. This stage typically lasts about two weeks for most songbirds.

## Leaving the nest

When songbird chicks are ready to leave the nest, they become increasingly active and eventually hop out onto a nearby branch or to the ground. Parent birds do

**Hatching**
*Breaking out of an egg is not easy for a tiny chick. A special, hard "egg tooth" develops on the end of its beak to help it nibble its way out and is then shed.*

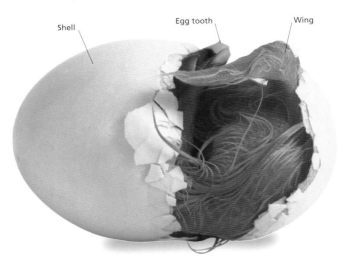

Shell

Egg tooth

Wing

**Fatherly feeding**
*Male House Wrens typically feed the chicks from their first nesting by themselves, while females lay a second clutch with a nearby male.*

not lure young out of the nest or "teach" their young to fly, but they keep providing food for many days after the chick leaves the nest. Nestlings encourage their parents to feed them by quivering their wings, displaying their vivid mouth patterns, and giving feeding calls.

## Abandoned birds

It is normal for fledglings of robins, jays, doves, and other birds to spend a few days on the ground before they can fly. These young are usually not abandoned, so they should be left alone—their parents are usually nearby so they do not need to be rescued.

## Baby birds

Once the chicks have become independent of their parents, their colorful mouth lining is no longer needed and fades.

**ABANDONED BIRDS?**
Young birds often look lost and vulnerable, but remember that the parents are probably not far away. Fledglings of species such as Blue Jays, American Robins and other thrushes, and Mourning Doves spend a day or two on the ground before they can fly. In most cases, the birds will be fine, so resist the urge to go to their aid.

**Baby birds**
*The colorful "gapes" encourage parents to put food in their mouths.*

# Migration

**About two-thirds of the species that nest in North America migrate at least a few hundred miles each spring and fall. Most winter on islands in the Caribbean and Central America, while some migrate as far as the southern tip of South America.**

## Why they do it

Birds must maintain a body temperature over 100° F (38° C) and their active lifestyle requires abundant and reliable food. Nearly all birds that nest in the northern latitudes of North America must leave in winter to find food. Birds repeat their dangerous journeys each spring to their nesting habitat because northern climates provide abundant food such as mosquitoes and blackflies, which are ideal for feeding their young. Northern habitats also have longer days, and fewer nest parasites and predators.

**Recent immigrant**
*European Starlings have already developed migratory habits in North America.*

## How they do it

Daytime migrants use visual landmarks such as rivers, but most small birds fly during the cool hours of night to avoid hawks and conserve water. Nocturnal migrants can orient themselves by constellations around the North Star and variations in the Earth's magnetic field. The ability to migrate is learned by some species, but is driven by an instinct in others such as thrushes, vireos, and warblers, the young of which migrate to ancestral winter homes without the company of their parents.

## Champion migrant

An occupant of barns in North America, some Barn Swallows migrate to Tierra del Fuego at the southern tip of South America.

**Welcome nourishment**
*Ripe crabapples provide fuel for this migrating Swainson's Thrush during its fall migration.*

**Long-distance champ**
*Among landbirds, the Barn Swallow and closely related Eurasian Swallow probably hold the migration record. Barn Swallows that nest in northern Canada may winter as far south as the tip of Argentina.*

# Feeding

**"Eating like a bird" could not be more misleading— in order to maintain their active lifestyle, small birds must eat one quarter of their weight daily. Some species have bills specialized to particular foods, but the diet of most varies with the time of year.**

## Importance of feeding

The best way to provide food for birds is to plant trees, shrubs, vines, and groundcovers. These can provide not only seeds and fruits but also insects, which all species need to feed their young. Such plantings can also provide nesting places, shelter during extreme weather, and singing perches.

**Citrus enthusiast**
*Baltimore Orioles are sometimes attracted by juicy citrus halves and by oriole-size nectar feeders.*

Well-established bird plantings can last for centuries, nurturing many generations of birds.

## Timing of feeding

Birds feed most often in the early morning and late afternoon. Feeding in the morning provides fuel after their nocturnal fast depletes reserves. Dependable food supplies are especially important for small birds such as chickadees,

**Earthworm specialist**
*American Robins can detect the slightest movement of earthworms and deftly extract them for a meal. Although they look like they are cocking their head to listen, this actually gives them a better view.*

which deplete most of their reserves during long winter nights. To survive low temperatures, birds eat much more on cold days than warm ones and migrants eat voraciously before embarking on their journeys. Females also increase the amount of food they eat when forming eggs, and will eat bits of crushed oyster shell or roasted eggshells as well, as a calcium supplement. During the nesting and molting seasons, most birds load their young with insects and other animal life because these foods are rich in protein, which is necessary for growing chicks.

## Natural food supplies

In addition to plantings, leaf mulch placed under shrubs and a brush pile created with fallen branches can also be used to attract birds to your backyard. Birds will scratch through the leaves and in the brush piles to pick up insects to nourish themselves and their families.

**Agile acrobat**
*White-breasted Nuthatches cling to trees upside down, peering into bark crevices for insects. They store food in caches and return later, using their chisel-like bills to hammer open nuts and seeds.*

### CACHING FOOD
Birds of all sizes store food that may be used during lean months. Jays, chickadees, titmice, and other seedeaters collect more seed at feeders than they can eat—and stash the excess for leaner days ahead. Clark's Nutcrackers, a western crow relative, can dig through 18 in (45 cm) of snow to retrieve cached seeds and nuts.

**Accidental planters**
*Jays also bury nuts for future use, some of which germinate and grow into oaks.*

■ **SEASONAL TIPS**
*There is much to enjoy in the backyard in spring, and plenty of "bird gardening" to keep you busy.*

**1 Food**
Clean up feeders and seed spilled underneath them. In April or May, hang a hummingbird feeder. Orange halves may attract orioles.

**2 Nest boxes**
Put up new nest boxes and remove last year's nests from older boxes. Provide short lengths of string, wool, and feathers for nest-building.

**3 Cover**
Spring is the best planting season. Select and plant native trees, shrubs, and vines, for year-round cover.

# Spring

**Resident birds arrive to set up nesting territories and migrants stop in for food, water, and rest. This is the time to enjoy birdsong and watch the courtship and family life of backyard birds.**

## Preparing to nest

Both resident and migratory birds grow a new set of body feathers in spring. Brightly colored males convey their health, age, and breeding condition with their new colors. Females select a mate largely on the appearance of the male and the strength of his song. Females also grow new feathers in spring and their appetite increases as eggs develop.

## Spring arrivals

Keep a daily journal describing the details of your backyard bird observations. Or make a list of the birds that you observe to compare arrival dates and the sequence of appearance from one year to the next.

### VITAL SPRING FOOD

In northern and mountain regions, March and April often bring heavy snowfall that can cover the ground for days and hide food. Trees and shrubs that retain their fruit through winter and well-stocked feeders help birds survive.

## SPRING BIRD PLUMAGE

**AMERICAN GOLDFINCH**

Males are yellow with a black cap

**INDIGO BUNTING**

Males are completely blue

**YELLOW-RUMPED WARBLER**

Males and females have bright yellow shoulders and rump

**Backyard thrush**
American Robins start nesting in early spring. Two weeks after hatching, the young will leave the nest and the parents will soon lay a second clutch.

■ SEASONAL TIPS
*Summer is the time to care for the new generation that have hatched in, or close to, your backyard.*

**1** Predator watch
Keep your cat indoors to help birds. This is especially important in the spring, when baby birds are on the ground for a few days before they can fly.

**2** Water
Keep a fresh supply of water available in your garden. Watch the color of the water and change it when necessary. Place your bird bath on a pedestal.

**3** Food caution
Avoid using suet during the summer because it will melt, staining feathers, and become rancid. If you feed hummingbirds, rinse the feeders once a week.

# Summer

**Backyard birds feed young and defend them from predators during this busy season. Young birds will still beg for food, although they are as large as their parents when they leave the nest.**

## Baby boom

Bird populations are at their highest in summer as nestlings join their parents. Some birds, such as American Crows and Barn Swallows, receive help raising their young from members of previous broods. These helpers gain experience in domestic responsibilities, while their veteran parents receive assistance.

## Tattered look

By late summer, parent birds may look frazzled from the work of raising their brood. Their feathers may look bleached and worn. In some, patches of feathers on the head and neck are replaced in a late summer molt, adding to the tattered look of parent birds.

### A HELPING HAND

Help parent birds provide meals for their young by placing mealworms in a steep-sided metal cake tray. Obtain mealworms at local pet shops or breed them in a tub filled with bran, a slice of apple for moisture, and covered with newspaper.

## SUMMER BIRD PLUMAGE

**TREE SWALLOW**

White below and glossy blue above

**HOUSE SPARROW**

Males have a black bib and gray crown

**SCARLET TANAGER**

Males are red with black wings and tail

**Colorful visitor**
*The male Painted Bunting summers in the Southeast, nesting in dense shrubs and sometimes eating millet at backyard feeders.*

■ SEASONAL TIPS
*Autumn is a good season to clean up birdfeeders and the spilled grain under the feeders.*

**1 Cleanup**
Clean birdfeeders to make them safe for wintering birds. Soak in a 10 percent solution of nonchlorinated bleach, then scrub and rinse thoroughly.

**2 Planting time**
With the threat of scorching summer days behind, autumn is a good season to plant trees such as crabapples, hawthorns, dogwoods, spruce, and pines.

**3 Leaves for birds**
Rake leaves under shrubs to create natural leaf mulch—ideal habitat for earthworms, spiders, and insects—and create a brush pile to provide shelter.

# Autumn

**In autumn, birds are building fat reserves to begin their migration and molting into sleek, fresh plumages. Young are leaving the care of their parents and migrating by themselves to their winter homes.**

## Stocking up

Food is plentiful in autumn—the abundant seed of wildflowers and grass, fruits, and insects. Birds select lipid-rich foods, such as spicebush, to help create the fat reserves needed for migration. Insects provide protein used in growing new feathers. As autumn progresses, migrants and overwintering birds gain valuable extra weight.

## Flocks

In autumn, blackbirds may form flocks that number in the hundreds of thousands. They land on fields offering abundant food that is easily obtained, and their vast numbers offer protection from predators such as hawks.

### THE NATURAL HARVEST

This is the season of greatest natural food abundance, so it is less important to offer food at birdfeeders. This is also the season of the highest numbers of birds, because both adults and the young of the year may visit your backyard.

## AUTUMN BIRD PLUMAGE

### ROSE-BREASTED GROSBEAK

Rose color fading on breast, soon replaced by beige with dark streaks

### AMERICAN GOLDFINCH

Lemon yellow body feathers are molted and replaced by olive feathers in autumn

**Oak planter**
*Many of the acorns stashed by Blue Jays for winter reserves are forgotten and grow to great oak trees, thereby providing food for future generations.*

■ **SEASONAL TIPS**
*Abundant cover such as conifers, dense shrubs, and brush piles offer shelter for wintering birds.*

**1 Birdfeeders**
This is the most useful season for birdfeeders, especially in northern climates where snow can cover natural food sources. Provide sunflower seeds and millet.

**2 Water source**
Provide open water in birdbaths. To prevent the water from freezing, install a water heater with a thermostat (these are available from birdfood stores).

**3 Getting ready**
Prepare for spring by creating a landscaping plan using native plants. Build birdhouses for the spring nesting season and install them by late March.

# Winter

**Birds that feed on conifer cones, such as finches, or on tree trunks, such as woodpeckers, stay through the winter. Most others move south beyond the reach of accumulating snow.**

## Winter flocks

The drive to defend nesting territories wanes during winter and flocks form. These winter flocks of hardy northern species, such as chickadees, nuthatches, and woodpeckers, roam together through the woods, constantly on the watch for both feeding opportunities and predators such as hawks.

## Coming in from the cold

Many birds fly south to avoid the extremes of more northern latitudes. Juncos and Tree Sparrows are common winter feeder birds. Sometimes there is an "irruption" of winter finches such as Common Redpolls and Pine Siskins, when their natural food sources fail.

### VITAL WINTER FOOD

In northern latitudes, provide beef fat suet on the coldest days. This helps birds replenish their fat reserves. Black-oil sunflower and nyger seeds also provide high calorie oils for wintering birds, especially in years when conifer seed crops fail.

## WINTER BIRD PLUMAGE

**BOHEMIAN WAXWING**

Rusty color under tail, white tips on wing feathers, beige crest

**PINE GROSBEAK**

Brick-red color, white wing bars, heavy bill

**COMMON REDPOLL**

Red crown, tiny bill, streaks on sides of breasts, black throat

**Winter insulation**
*On cold days, this female Cardinal traps body heat by fluffing her feathers. On cold nights she tucks her bill into her feathers.*

# Birds in the backyard

There are many things you can do to attract birds to your backyard. Provide nest boxes, water, and food, and cultivate bird-friendly plants.

# Backyard habitats

**Bird gardeners should try to mimic natural habitats in the backyard. Good habitats provide food, cover, nesting places, and perches. Property owners that succeed provide a valuable refuge for both resident and migratory birds.**

## Think about layers

Natural habitats consist of many layers: groundcover, small shrubs, tall shrubs, understory trees, and canopy trees—all linked together with twining vines. These layers are important because birds prefer to feed, nest, and sing at different heights from the ground—hence a backyard that has a number of layers will meet the feeding and nesting needs of the greatest variety of species. Densely layered habitats have more leaf surfaces that provide food for insects—and the more insects, the more birds. Such habitats also provide better cover in which birds can hide from predators and seek shelter during extreme weather.

**Backyard bird sanctuary**
*The ideal sanctuary provides plants for food, shelter, and nesting. It also offers water and food throughout the year.*

## Be a messy gardener

Natural habitats are not tidy places—so resist the temptation to rake, cut, and trim every dead branch and dried flowerhead. Dead limbs and even trees are important to birds.

## Go native

When deciding which plants to buy at your local nursery, ask the owner for advice on native plants that grow well in your area. In general, plants that are native to your state or province are better adapted to the extremes of local climate and can thrive during droughts and freezes that

**Health food**
*Earthworms are a good food for nestling birds. Avoid yard pesticides to keep them a safe meal.*

would kill most exotic plants. Similarly, check that plants will tolerate the specific conditions in your backyard—sun or shade, wet or dry and well-drained soil. As our climate changes due to global warming, native plants are more likely to survive than exotics, although some may also thrive under the right conditions. Some exotic plants can also become invasive, creating a "monoculture" that is dominated by a single species. Japanese barberry, tatarian honeysuckle, Oriental bittersweet, and Norway maple are all invasives.

A small backyard pond will provide an additional magnet for birds, and will also attract frogs, dragonflies and other insects, and the birds that feed on them.

**Water feature**
*A pool can provide bathing and drinking water for birds and a home for frogs and other wetland animals.*

**Natural food source**
*Native fruiting shrubs such as this highbush cranberry viburnum provide nutritious food at useful times of year— and it is just the right size to swallow.*

# Natural food and shelter

**Plants benefit birds by providing food, nesting places, and shelter during extreme weather—and birds benefit plants by pollinating their flowers and distributing their seeds. More than 300 kinds of plants depend on birds to disperse their seeds.**

## Attractive fruits

Plants dependent on birds to distribute their seeds typically have bright colored fruits or leaves when seeds are ready. Bright colors alert birds that fruit is ready to eat.

When seeds are ready for dispersal, the fruits of bird-distributed plants provide "bait" to make their fruit appealing, usually sugar or fat. Fruit ripening usually coincides with the migrations of North American birds. Most bird-distributed fruits ripen as the peak number of birds moves south in the autumn. Likewise, fruit size is associated with particular birds. Few native fruits are larger than ½ inch (1.3 cm), a convenient size for thrushes, mockingbirds, and waxwings to swallow.

**Multitasking plants**
*Plant a nectar-rich flower border like this one to encourage insects. A native wildflower mix will bear seeds for birds.*

## Planting for the seasons

Shrubs, vines, and trees that meet the needs of birds can be planted throughout the year. Here are some suggestions:

**Spring** Foods with high sugar content, such as mulberries, raspberries, serviceberries, and black cherries are often fed to nestling birds.

**Summer** Late-ripening fruits with high sugar content are readily eaten by both fledglings and adults. High-sugar fruits include blackberries, huckleberries, grapes, and blueberries.

**Autumn** Fruits that produce lipids converted to fat are valuable

**Thistle eater**
*American Goldfinches eat thistle seeds and use them to line their nests.*

**Dogwood display**
*The abundant fruit of the native flowering dogwood helps birds to build fat for migration.*

## NATURAL PEST CONTROL

Try not to be too tidy when gardening. Let some grass grow long, and leave a patch of wildflowers—they provide seeds and attract insects for birds to eat. Don't trim back shrubs too early and leave berries intact as a food source throughout winter. Avoid chemical pesticide—birds provide natural pest control.

for migration since fats yield twice as much energy as carbohydrates or proteins. High-lipid fruits include spicebush, sassafras, magnolia, and flowering dogwood.

**Winter** Fruits that persist on trees through winter offer carbohydrates. To provide winter and early spring fruits, plant hawthorns, crabapples, viburnums, and mountain-ash.

**Bunchberry**
*Ruffed Grouse and thrushes such as Veery and Wood Thrush feed on plump clusters of bunchberry in the autumn.*

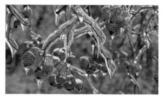

**Washington Hawthorn**
*Some trees hold their fruit through winter and spring, providing food for robins, flickers, and mockingbirds.*

# Bird-friendly lawns

**The close-cropped lawns that dominate most backyards are a relatively sterile habitat that is used by few birds. Those that do venture onto lawns may be injured or killed by chemical treatments such as insecticides and herbicides.**

## Less lawn

Lawn provides little food and no cover for birds. To make your backyard a more bird-friendly habitat, reduce the size of your lawn by at least 25 percent and replace it with a wildflower meadow. The simplest way to reduce your lawn and encourage wildflowers is to just stop mowing along the back edge of your property—then the wildflowers that were suppressed by the mower can have a chance to grow. If the wildflowers are left to go to seed, they form a natural food source for birds and there will also be more butterflies and insects available for birds to eat and feed to their young.

In the United States, home owners use about 8 pounds of pesticide/acre (9 kg/hectare)—three times more than used by farmers. This poison kills about 67 million birds each year. Pesticides are unnecessary lawn additives, threatening not only birds but the children that play in yards. Community water supplies are also affected because lawn chemicals find their way into the groundwater and nearby streams and lakes. Organic pesticides are still poisons, and may affect insects and the birds that eat them.

**Native Bee Balm**
*A favorite nectar source for birds and bees; a winter-hardy perennial that is easy to grow.*

**Trumpet Honeysuckle**
*A climbing vine for trellis and fences, this provides summer nectar in its tube-shaped flowers and red fruit in autumn.*

**Red Flowering Currant**
*This deciduous, prickly, drought-resistant shrub provides nectar, nesting cover, and sweet fruit in late summer.*

**Ocotillo**
*A native, thorny shrub of warm desert regions, this provides nectar and insects in spring and grows best in full sun.*

## Leaf compost

Rake leaves under shrubs rather than burning or bagging them for municipal pickups. When leaves are left to decompose, they form ideal mulch beds where juncos, towhees, thrashers, and wrens can find reliable sources of insect food.

## Brush piles

When heavy winds, rains, or snows break off branches from your trees

**Hummingbird favorite**
*Salvias are among the favorite garden plants for Ruby-throated Hummingbirds. The deep flowers provide sweet nectar.*

and shrubs, pile them into a heap in a back corner of your yard to create a brush pile. This shelter is readily used by backyard birds during the extreme heat of summer and in cold and stormy weather during the winter and early spring.

**Raking leaves**
*Leaves that are left to compost under shrubs serve a double purpose: they provide insect food for birds and the mulch effect helps the shrub.*

# Feeders

**Feed birds throughout the year and you will enjoy a procession of species that changes with the seasons. Although feeding birds brings birds up close for amazing views, it comes with a responsibility to protect them from collision with windows, attacks from cats, and exposure to disease.**

## Bird tables

The simplest way to provide food for birds is to place food on an open table that is covered to keep off rain and snow. Bird tables should have adequate drainage to prevent food from getting soggy and a raised lip to prevent the seed from blowing away. Elevated feeders help keep birds safe from cats while bringing birds to eye level.

## Suet feeders

In colder months, suet is an excellent source of fat and is readily eaten by woodpeckers, chickadees, titmice, and nuthatches. Provide the suet in a hanging bag or feeder well above the reach of neighborhood dogs and raccoons.

**Covered bird table**
*This pole-mounted bird table has a sturdy base and a roof to keep food dry. The tray is removable for easy cleaning.*

**Suet feeder**
*The sparrow-sized Downy Woodpecker readily clings to suet hanging from a tree limb. Avoid pounding nails into trees, which causes unnecessary damage.*

**Hanging hummer feeder**
*Hummingbirds feed at flowers from ground level up to the tallest trees, so they are quick to visit hanging feeders. The red color helps attract these birds.*

Suet should not be offered during warm weather (80°F/27°C or higher) because it may melt, staining feathers and affecting their waterproofing, and turn rancid.

## Window alert

About one billion birds die each year after hitting windows. To reduce the chance of a window collision near your feeders, cover the window with screens or create a window cover from fruit tree netting so that birds will not strike the glass. To minimize the risk of a lethal collision, position feeders within 3 feet (90cm) of a window or more than 30 feet (9m) away. Birds that have been startled from feeders located close to windows by a hawk or other disturbance will usually not have gathered up enough momentum for a lethal collision. In spring, robins and cardinals can chase their own reflections against windows. To prevent this, hang wind chimes or other distractions over the trouble spots, or attach translucent stickers.

**Ground-feeding table**
*Ground feeders attract both birds that typically feed on the ground, such as this Blue Jay, and those that feed in trees and shrubs.*

## Hanging feeders

Finches, chickadees, titmice, and many other species typically hang from trees and bushes as they search for food, so coming to a hanging feeder is second nature to these birds. Hanging feeders have the advantage of protecting the seed from burial under snow, and they can help to keep birds safe from attacks by cats and other predators.

Tube-shaped feeders typically consist of a plastic tube that comes in a variety of sizes. These feeders can store up to a week's worth of seed. Metal

**Peanut feeder**
*White-breasted Nuthatches, woodpeckers, chickadees, and titmice are attracted by a meal of hulled peanuts.*

portals set into the tubes are just the right size for dispensing either sunflower or nyger (sometimes called thistle) seed—a favorite finch food. Some tube-shaped feeders are also equipped with perches that are readily used by finches and other birds.

**Flock feeder**
*American Goldfinches usually occur in small flocks. Here they find abundant perches and food at a nyger seed feeder designed to cater for many visitors.*

### HYGIENE ALERT

Mold can grow in accumulated food under feeders. Rake up discarded seed and dispose of it in the garbage. Clean tube feeders in the spring and fall by soaking them in a 10 percent solution of non-chlorinated bleach. Scrub with a bottle brush and rinse thoroughly.

**Hanging feeders**
*The metal mesh on this feeder excludes squirrels and chipmunks, but is ideal for small-billed birds such as this siskin.*

## Squirrels

There are many feeders designed to deter squirrels from raiding food that you have set out for birds. The simplest designs center on providing a deterrent below the feeder, such as an inverted metal cone. In others, the weight of the squirrel causes the feeder to tip or close. Others keep squirrels and large birds away by putting the feeder inside a cage. Squirrels are notable for their persistence, agility, and intelligence, so keeping feeders totally free of squirrel raids is rare.

The best way to deter squirrels is to place feeders on an isolated post, far from buildings and overhanging branches. Although squirrels can leap several feet off the ground, they are even better at dropping onto feeders from above.

**Millet**
*The first choice of most sparrows, juncos, and buntings—small-billed birds that usually can't open larger seeds.*

**Sunflower seed**
*Striped and black oil sunflower seeds are the favorite choice for large-billed birds such as cardinals and grosbeaks.*

# Siting feeders

**Be sure to place bird feeders in locations where you can easily observe the birds you attract.**

**Optimum placement**
*With a bit of planning, you can position several types of feeders around your garden. If a feeder proves unpopular with the birds, move it around until you find a more suitable site.*

## Feeder placement

When considering a location to hang feeders, always place them where birds can easily escape if threatened by a hawk or cat. A good location typically gives the bird a clear view in all directions and provides a shrub or tree 6–9 feet (1.8–2.7 m) away from the feeder. Bird feeders should be positioned within 3 feet (1 m) or more than 30 feet (9 m) from a window to minimize the risk of window collisions. If ground feeders are used, they should have a wire mesh basket over them that permits small birds to enter, but keeps out larger birds and prevents predators from having access to birds while they are feeding.

*Bird tables can also be suspended from tree branches with secure chains.*

*Timid species such as cardinals will use low bird tables. Place them close to cover so the birds feel secure.*

**Wall feeder**
*Bird tables like this one can be mounted to walls. If birds are frightened from such locations, they usually do not gain enough momentum to hurt themselves against windows.*

**KEY**

- ☐ Ground feeders
- ☐ Bird tables
- ☐ Hanging feeders

A caged feeder at ground level is best positioned in an exposed spot so that birds can see predators approaching.

For a good view of the birds coming to your bird table, place it close to your house.

Pole-mounted feeders are easily moved, so find the birds' preferred spot.

Hanging tube feeders can be suspended from tree branches. Ensure threats are minimized.

**The natural look**
*American Goldfinches readily take sunflower seeds from this feeder.*

## BIRDFEEDER THREATS

Outdoor cats are one of the biggest threats to the safety of backyard birds as birds make up about 25 percent of their diet. They kill hundreds of millions of birds in North America every year. Position feeders and bird baths near prickly bushes such as raspberries to offer good cover for birds attempting to escape.

**Natural predator**
*Attaching a bell to a cat's quick-release collar will help alert birds to its presence.*

# Other foods

**Only a few birds eat seeds and grains, but many species may be attracted to your backyard if you provide suet, fruit, and other foods that you can buy or make.**

## Suet

Suet (usually beef kidney fat) is available at most grocery stores. It can be melted down and poured into cupcake tins or other containers to provide it in a convenient shape and size. Suet may also be placed in holes drilled into hanging logs. Raw suet is best offered by hanging chunks in mesh bags from garden hooks or tree branches. Suet mixes with everything from sunflower seeds to orange rinds are on sale, but they are less appealing to birds than a simple, solid block of plain suet. Do not offer suet once temperatures exceed 80°F (27°C) because melting suet can become rancid as well as staining bird feathers. Suet is

**Quick feeder**
*A hanging log with suet packed into any holes can be used as a feeder in the winter.*

readily eaten by chickadees, titmice, woodpeckers, and nuthatches.

## Summer foods

A mix of 1 part peanut butter, 4 parts cornmeal, 1 part flour, and 1 part vegetable shortening can be substituted for suet in warmer weather, and may attract tanagers, thrushes, and warblers.

Warm weather is also the season to offer fresh citrus. To attract orioles and tanagers, place half of an orange on a nail.

**Valuable food source**
*Birds are not too proud or fussy to take advantage of our leftovers. Many garden birds, including White-breasted Nuthatches, will eat kitchen scraps.*

When birds are feeding their young or bringing their new family to your feeders, offer them mealworms (beetle larvae). Mealworms can be obtained at your local pet shop or ordered online.

## Hummingbirds

Hummingbirds feed on flower nectar and the insects and small spiders that they find in flowers. Supplemental feeding of humming-birds may be useful to keep them in your yard until flowers bloom, or as a lure to entice hummingbirds into better viewing areas.

**Outdoor dining**
*Hummingbirds can be attracted to a nectar feeder—a large feeder like this one may even serve as a cafeteria for several hummingbirds at once.*

Keep hummingbird feeders clear of fungus by cleaning them every 2 or 3 days under hot running tapwater, scrubbing thoroughly with a bottlebrush. Although honey water is more nutritious than granular sugar water, it ferments faster in the sun than sugar water and cultures mold that can kill hummingbirds.

To prepare a sugar water solution, mix white or brown sugar and water together in equal (1:1) proportion, then boil the mixture to retard fermentation and dissolve all sugar. Dilute it with 4 parts cold water to 1 part solution when first attracting hummingbirds, but decrease the proportion to 1 part solution to 6 parts water after they learn the location of your feeders and flower gardens. Store the unused quantity in a refrigerator. Do not use red food coloring—it is not necessary as long as there are some red parts to the hummingbird feeder.

**Mealworms**
*Insects are a key food for nestling birds. Mealworms in a steep-sided metal baking pan will attract towhees, catbirds, thrashers, and bluebirds.*

**Raisins**
*Many birds are attracted to raisins, including mockingbirds and blackbirds.*

**Fruit**
*Any fruit that is starting to soften or brown can be cut up and put out on a tray.*

# Water

**Birds are readily attracted to water for both drinking and bathing—especially during the summer—but they will use it throughout the year if you keep the water clean and ice-free.**

**Keeping clean**
*Birds like this Scarlet Tanager can often be seen taking a bath. They are meticulous in their grooming.*

## Water safety

The simplest way to provide water is in a birdbath. Although birdbaths are readily available at most garden supply stores, most are more ornamental than practical because the bowl is too deep—birds usually bathe in a water puddle. Shallow water is key because a bird can dip into water and let it run over its back. Birds don't stay in the water long and don't get soaked to the skin, which would make them vulnerable to predators. Natural waterproofing usually keeps them from looking wet.

Birdbaths on pedestals are the safest way to provide water—especially where outdoor cats occur. It's helpful to put a dead tree branch next to the birdbath to provide a convenient perch where the bird can briefly land and inspect the surroundings for safety. Scrub out the bowl every few days with a stiff brush—especially during warm months to prevent mosquitoes from breeding in the water—and never use detergents.

Birdbaths equipped with dripper devices or sprays are especially attractive—but avoid gushing water, which will frighten birds rather than attract them. In northern latitudes, birdbaths equipped with heaters are useful for providing open water in winter.

**Easy access**
*Shallow edges enable birds, such as this Mourning Dove, to come and drink with their feet still firmly on the ground.*

**Bathing in safety**
*An elevated birdbath allows you to watch birds easily and keeps them safe from marauding cats.*

# Nest boxes

**Many species that formerly nested in natural cavities of tree trunks now compete with European Starlings and House Sparrows for those holes. Providing nest boxes is the simplest way to attract cavity-nesting birds.**

## Classic nest box

The classic, front-opening box is the best choice for most birds. Many species, including chickadees, titmice, Tree Swallows, and Great Crested Flycatchers, will use a birdhouse that is tailored for a bluebird. When the box dimensions are increased, even Screech-Owls and Wood Ducks will use this design. Owls and kestrels and several other species prefer several inches of large wood chips in the bottom of the box.

**Welcome home**
*Since nesting cavities in trees are scarce, many birds—including Eastern Bluebirds—raise their families in nest boxes.*

## Martin houses

Almost all Purple Martins now nest in artificial housing. Large wooden and metal houses with multiple apartments are still widely used, but the best choice is heavy-grade plastic gourds that are specially

**Valuable real estate**
*A well-placed Tree Swallow house will hold just one pair of nesting swallows, so the first pair to arrive at the site has the edge over latecomers.*

**Martin mansion**
*Nearly all Purple Martins in North America reside in human-built housing. Established colonies typically return to the same house for many years.*

designed for the purpose. These are available from the Purple Martin Conservation Association, at www.purplemartin.org.

## Open shelf structures

Birds that typically nest in caves and under porch roofs often accept nest shelves as a substitute. Robins, phoebes, and Barn Swallows readily accept open-faced nest shelves positioned under the eves of sheds and houses. The base should be 6 x 6 in (15 x 15 cm) for phoebes and swallows and 6 x 8 in (15 x 20 cm) for robins. A few sprigs of evergreen needles, such as arborvitae, stapled to the face of robin nest shelves may increase acceptance of the platform. To keep bird excrement from splattering below, install a larger board under the platform.

**Native condos**
*Native Americans used gourds as martin houses. After the nesting season, clean plastic gourds and store until early spring.*

## Christmas wreaths

Evergreen Christmas wreaths are an excellent support for nesting American Robins, House Finches, and juncos, all of which typically nest in trees and shrubs. Once the holiday season is over, move the wreath from the front door to a more secluded wall so that it will be ready for use by birds in the spring.

# Making nest boxes

**Birds will nest in a variety of wood, metal, plastic, and ceramic houses, but wood is the best material for durability, insulation, and ease of construction. A bluebird house can be constructed from a single board.**

## Construction tips

The best materials for building standard bluebird-size nest boxes are 1 x 8 inch (25 x 200mm) pine, spruce, or poplar boards. Cedar is more weather tolerant, but much more expensive. Avoid pressure-treated woods because they are impregnated with toxic chemicals such as arsenic. The size of the entrance hole is very important because it can keep out starlings. The diameter used for Eastern and Western Bluebirds—1½ inch (38mm)—is ideal for many species.

## Positioning boxes

Face nest box entrances to the east in cold-weather climates. This warms the box by exposing the broad face of the box to morning sunlight. In southern states, the east-facing position is not as important. Mount boxes about 4 feet (1.2m) off the ground on a stand-alone pole to reduce the risk of predation.

## Cleaning nest boxes

It is essential to clean nest boxes in early spring in order to remove old bird and mouse nests, as well as to help control parasitic insects, mites, and lice. Nest boxes with a swing-out front or side are easiest to clean. In this design, the front wall simply pivots on two nails and is secured to the base with a single screw. Use a spatula or ice scraper to clean out the box.

**Nest box height**
*Attach nest boxes to a firm structure about 4–5 feet (1.2–1.5m) off the ground. Fences and fence posts are excellent locations.*

**Maintenance**
*New nest boxes (left) will naturally weather and last for years. Avoid painted or pressure-treated wood.*

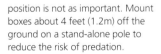

## HOW TO BUILD A NEST BOX

Use the dimensions shown in this plan for this classic wooden birdhouse. Mark the entrance hole using a compass and drill it to size. Use 1½ inch (38mm) galvanized screws to assemble the parts and leave the wood untreated for the birds' safety.

### Materials

❶ Pine, spruce, poplar, or cedar board—3 feet (1m) long, 1in (25mm) thick, and 9¼in (235mm) wide
❷ Two 1½in (38mm) aluminum nails for side door pivot; galvanized screws

Before assembly, drill a small attachment hole at the top and the bottom of the back panel.

7½ in (190 mm)

9¼ in (230 mm)

5 in (130 mm)

9¼ in (230 mm)

5 in (130)

1½ in (38 mm)

9¼in (230 mm)

4 in (130 mm)

5 in (127mm)

6½ in (165 mm)

5 x 5 in (130 x 130 mm)

To keep predators from reaching through the entrance hole, place it 7¾in (200mm) above the floor of the box. A 4 x 5in (100 x 130mm) block of wood with a hole size the same as the entrance gives added protection.

### Completed nest box

*Secure the box to a tree or wall with a screw at the top and another at the bottom.*

# How to identify

Consider the following ten clues when identifying birds: shape, posture, flight patterns, field marks, size, color, behavior, habitat, season, and song.

# Anatomy

**An understanding of basic bird anatomy is the first step to identifying birds. Learning the parts of birds and the names of feathers is helpful because these words are used to describe species in field guides.**

## Shape and posture

Taxonomists have organized the approximately 800 species of North American birds into 27 families. Birds within each family have similar shape and posture when sitting and many species have distinctive flight patterns.

For example, most woodpeckers have a distinctive shape with large bill, and are often seen with their tail propped against tree trunks. Learn to recognize birds by the unique shapes, postures, and flight patterns of each family.

## Adaptations for flight

The same names are used for feathers and other body regions whether the bird is as small as a hummingbird or as large as a condor. Learn these names once, then apply them to all species.

underwing coverts

forehead

bill

axillary feathers

flank

chin

throat

breast

belly

**Coverts**
*The feathers covering the base of the primaries, secondaries, and tail feathers are present on the dorsal as well as the ventral side, and are called the primary, secondary, and uppertail coverts respectively.*

undertail coverts

feet

tail

## Contour feathers

A bird's body is covered with small feathers that are known as contour feathers. Songbirds the size of a sparrow may have as many as 2,500 body feathers (not counting underlying down feathers) in winter and about 1,500 in summer. Even a tiny hummingbird may have 1,000 feathers. Birds can look very different from one season to the next, and they change their appearance as they mature. All feathers are shed (molted) and replaced at least once each year. Most contour feathers have a downy base and a stiffer vane that is formed by interlocking barbs creating a smooth surface. Birds also have hundreds of down feathers that provide insulation in cool weather and at night.

**Wing feathers**
*Each region of the wing is characterized by feathers of a different shape and type. The primaries and secondaries are single rows of stiff feathers, covered at their base by four rows of small contour feathers, known as underwing coverts.*

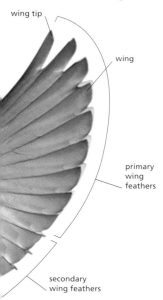

wing tip

wing

primary
wing
feathers

secondary
wing feathers

### BIRD SENSES

Owls have excellent vision and can turn their heads about 270 degrees. The disk-shaped face traps and filters sound waves toward ears, which are hidden. This process gives owls particularly good hearing, allowing them to detect the faint sounds of mice and other prey. The Barred Owl visits backyards, although you are more likely to hear one calling at night than to see it.

## Bird anatomy

Birds are the only animals with feathers—highly specialized structures that allow them to fly, stay warm, and communicate information about age, sex, and health. The types of feathers and parts of a bird's anatomy are labeled on this Bohemian Waxwing.

## Flight feathers

The strong, stiff primaries and secondaries enable birds to propel themselves; tail feathers help with balance and changing direction.

# Plumages and field marks

**Birds typically molt all of their feathers over the course of a year, giving them different looks by season and age. Careful attention to distinctive plumages and marks on the face, breast, wings, and tail can help birders recognize closely related species.**

## Changing appearances

Many species show great variation in plumages between males and females. For example, male and female Baltimore Orioles and Red-winged Blackbirds look so different that one might think the males and females belonged to different species. In contrast, there are few differences in the plumages of male, female, and juvenile crows, magpies, and jays. Juvenile birds can look very different from their parents. For example, a young male Orchard Oriole has a black throat that makes it look like a different species. Some birds change from summer to winter. By the end of the summer, most small birds have worn feathers and replace them by molting before they migrate. Some migrants, like vireos and flycatchers, look the same all year, but others molt from brilliant spring colors to drab, camouflaged plumages in the autumn—just before they migrate to the tropics. Year-round residents such as chickadees and wrens also molt, but they look the same throughout the year.

**Vivid male**
*This male Baltimore Oriole is an easy bird to identify; the female is a much paler version and lacks the black head.*

## FEATHER CARE

Birds must keep their plumage in excellent condition in order to retain their ability to fly. Exposure to sun and wind dries the feathers and makes them brittle. To lubricate and maintain their feathers, birds spend hours each day preening themselves with lubricating oil rubbed from their preen gland, which is located over the tail.

## Field marks

The detailed patterns on their head, wings, tail, and breast help birds recognize other members of their species. Birders who learn to quickly search for distinguishing field marks can use them to distinguish similar species. Watch for eye rings, eye stripes, wing bars, outer tail patterns, rump color, and other details as these make species identifications more certain.

**YOUNG STARLING**

**ADULT STARLING**

**JAY**

**SCREECH-OWL**

**Identifying feathers**
*The base (shaft) of nestlings' flight feathers are usually wrapped in a white sheath. Color may change with the angle of viewing. Owl feathers, soft along the vane, allow silent flight.*

**Pine Grosbeak**
*Although similar to the Purple Finch, the Pine Grosbeak can be distinguished by its redder plumage with two white wing bars and its much larger size.*

# Color and size

**When faced with an unknown bird, its color and size are important clues to identification, but beware, these clues are influenced by distance and lighting, both of which give the illusion of larger body size.**

## Color

The brilliant colors of birds would seem to be a logical way to identify them, but color is very tricky, being totally dependent on the angle of the light. For example, an Indigo Bunting is a brilliant blue from belly to head and back, but the bird often appears completely black because of backlighting. Color also varies with time of year, age, and gender. Usually only breeding males show brilliant colors, and only in the nesting season when viewed with optimal lighting. Different artists bring their own style and color palate to their art, while the color in photographic guides may be especially misleading because they illustrate individuals in the lighting of the moment.

**Neighborhood watch**
*Watch your garden birds regularly and you will get to know their behavior and body types. Compare them with one another to help with identification.*

## Size

Size is most useful when comparing a mystery bird to a known bird. Three common birds—House Sparrow, American Robin, and American Crow—can serve as useful references, especially if the mystery bird is nearby. For example, both Black-capped Chickadees and House Sparrows have black "bibs" (throat and upper breast), but the chickadee is much smaller than a House Sparrow. Likewise, Hairy Woodpeckers are about the size of a robin and the look-alike Downy Woodpecker is the size of a sparrow. Beware of using size for identifying birds at a distance without known-sized birds or structures for comparison.

**BLACK-CAPPED CHICKADEE**

**HOUSE SPARROW**

**AMERICAN CROW**

**AMERICAN ROBIN**

# Bills and tails

**The shape of a bird's bill is often a solid clue to its family relationship, suggesting adaptations to specific foods. Tails can also be helpful for clinching identifications. Shapes, color patterns, and behavior such as tail-flicking are all helpful clues.**

## Bills

Bill shapes can reveal relationships. For example, woodpeckers all have stout, well-reinforced bills that let them dig into wood, while thrushes varying from bluebirds to robins have similar-shaped bills with a small hook that helps them hold insects, worms, and snail shells. Likewise, finches, sparrows, juncos, and towhees all have seed-cracking bills that convey close relationships. Because most field guides organize birds by relationships, observation of

**Balancing act**
*The long, forked tail of the Barn Swallow trails out behind it in flight and helps with balance on trees and wires. Its tiny bill is adapted for eating insects.*

bill shape can be very helpful, permitting the unknown bird to be placed in a family.

## Tails

Tail shapes are important for aiding flight, but they are also billboards for displaying a bird's identity, age, and fitness. Some similar species such as Barn and Cliff Swallows

**FINCH SKULL**

**WOODPECKER SKULL**

**Seedeater**
*This strong and powerful bill is used for cracking nuts and seeds.*

**HARD SEEDS**

**Precision tool**
*This bill is long and chisel-like for finding beetles and grubs among bark.*

**BEETLE**

**THRUSH SKULL**

**KESTREL SKULL**

**Multipurpose bill**
*This bill can tackle fruit and all kinds of invertebrates, from worms to snails.*

**SNAIL SHELL**

**Meat-eater**
*This sharp bill has a hooked tip for seizing small mammals and tearing flesh.*

**MEAT STRIP**

have similar body shapes, but vary greatly in the shape of their tails. Barn Swallows, for example, have deeply forked tails, and males display longer outer tail feathers than females. In contrast, both male and female Cliff Swallows have short, square-tipped tails. Even the tips of tails can serve as helpful marks. Bohemian and Cedar Waxwings have yellow tail tips and Eastern Kingbirds flash white-tipped tails. Some birds also hold their tails in distinctive ways, such as wrens that may cock their tail upward and phoebes that pump their tails up and down. Many hawk species have color or distinctive banding in their tails as adults, but the young of these

**Yellow-tipped tail**
*The yellow tip on the tail is one of the distinctive field marks for both Cedar and Bohemian (above) Waxwings.*

species lack distinctive tail marking. For example, Red-tailed Hawks are named for the rusty-red tail of the adult, but first-year birds have a gray tail instead.

# Range, season, & habitat

Range, season, and habitat are helpful considerations for identifying similar species. Although birds sometimes show up in surprising places at odd times of the year, most of the time they are remarkably predictable in their occurrence.

## Range

Although most birds move from summer to winter homes, their annual movements occur within well-defined ranges from which they seldom stray. Even long-distance migrants have predictable summer and winter homes with reliable migration routes and stopovers.

Those new to birding should pay special attention to learning the usual ranges of species that are common in their area. Then, if a bird is seen outside its normal range, it will be more obvious.

Ranges are especially helpful for identifying similar species. For example, Eastern and Western Meadowlarks are very similar in appearance, but their ranges rarely overlap. With climates becoming warmer, ranges of birds will change, with southern species such as Red-bellied Woodpecker, Tufted Titmouse, and Turkey Vulture expanding northward.

**Winter visitor**
*American Tree Sparrows are a common bird at backyard feeders in northern states during winter.*

**Anna's Hummingbird**
*This West Coast hummingbird is the most common hummingbird at backyard gardens during the winter months.*

**Eastern Meadowlark**
*Robin-sized meadowlarks frequent large grassy fields and are seldom found in backyards or other habitats.*

**Chipping Sparrow**
*Several sparrows have rusty colored caps, but the Chipping Sparrow also has a black line through its eyes.*

**Swamp Sparrow**
*Freshwater marshes are the favorite haunt for Swamp Sparrows, which lack the Chipping Sparrow's black eye line.*

## Season

Migratory birds return to their usual nesting places at the same time each year because the urge to migrate is triggered by seasonal changes in day length. This helps ensure that they arrive when food supplies are adequate, especially important for birds that rely on aquatic food and flying insects.

## Habitat

Birders can use the preferred habitats of birds to help distinguish between similar species. For example, Swamp, Field, and Chipping Sparrows all have gray breasts and rusty red crowns. Although their ranges overlap during the same seasons in many locations, these three species have very distinct habitat preferences. Chipping Sparrows are common around residential neighborhoods, but you are unlikely to see either Field or Swamp Sparrows in your backyard because Field Sparrows live in brushy fields, and Swamp Sparrows prefer the edges of freshwater marshes and wetlands.

# Watching

**Most birders recall a single encounter that sparked a lifelong fascination with birds and led to further activities and discoveries.**

## When to watch

Songbirds are most active in the early hours of the day. After a night of fasting, birds are hungry and visit feeders in the greatest numbers. Morning is also the time of greatest song, as birds reestablish their territories.

By midday, birds are less active and use their time largely for feather maintenance. There is also an evening peak in feeding activity as birds stock up for their nocturnal fast. Evening is also a good time to watch for birds returning to their roosts; some may gather in the hundreds of thousands.

## Basic tools

Having made the effort to attract birds to your backyard, you will want to be able to reap the benefits.

**Watching bird behavior**
*Birdfeeders are a great place to observe bird behavior. Here a male Downy Woodpecker vies for a meal with House Sparrows.*

Binoculars and field identification guides are the primary tools for enjoying birds. Binoculars will bring the birds close enough that you can identify them with the aid of one or more field guides. Although there are many kinds of binoculars available, the general rule is to purchase a pair with a magnification of about 8 power and an objective lens about 40 (the distance in mm across the large lens). Binoculars with higher magnification are difficult to hold steady, and those

**Natural camouflage**
*Shy birds such as waterflowl may fly or swim away as you approach. If you can, stay hidden when watching birds.*

with smaller than a 40-objective lens may not provide enough light.

## Getting the best view

If you have put careful thought into the positioning of your feeders, bird tables, and nest boxes, you will have a clear view of the birds in your backyard. Watching from the inside, you have the perfect "blind"—a shelter that enables you to see the birds without them seeing you—because they can't discern your outline through the window. Try to keep noise to a minimum and avoid sudden movements.

The longer a feeder has been in place, the more comfortable birds will feel using it, and they will become used to your presence.

### KEEPING RECORDS

Keeping lists of the birds at your feeders and in your backyard is both fun and a great way to contribute to bird conservation. When you participate in eBird and the Great Backyard Bird Count, your data is pooled with other local counts across the country to identify species at risk.

**Counting**
*A hand clicker is a great way to tally birds for eBird and the Great Backyard Bird Count. The numbers are combined and contrasted with other birders' observations.*

# Bird profiles

## KEY TO SYMBOLS

♀ female    ♂ male

☾ juvenile    ◐ immature
● adult

⚡ spring    ☼ summer
❄ fall    ❋ winter

## SCALE INDICATORS

Each species is compared to an average sized hand, to give an accurate indication of its size.

7in (18cm)

## DISTRIBUTION MAPS

Each species profile includes a map showing the range of the species, with four colors reflecting the bird's seasonal location.

▮ Summer distribution

▮ Resident all year

▮ Seen on migration

▮ Winter distribution

# Cooper's Hawk

*Accipiter cooperii*

The Cooper's Hawk is attracted to groups of smaller birds that gather around garden birdfeeders. Like the rest of its family, this medium-sized woodland hawk has a distinctive flight pattern of several quick flaps followed by a glide. Long legs and talons help it to capture ground-feeding birds in dense brush.

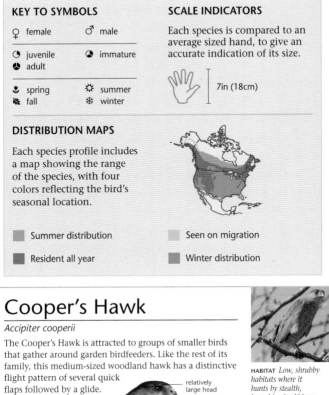

relatively large head

rust colored underparts

long, rounded tail

gray tail with wide, dark bands

white band at tip of tail

**HABITAT** *Low, shrubby habitats where it hunts by stealth, launching itself from hidden perches.*

brown barring on breast

**VOICE** *A rapid, barking kek, kek, kek; also long keeee (male), or waaaa (female).*
**NESTING** *In tall woodlands and along rivers; 3–6 eggs; 1 brood; April–May.*
**FEEDING** *Eats ground-feeding birds, small mammals, and reptiles.*
**SIMILAR SPECIES** *Sharp-shinned Hawk, Northern Goshawk.*

# Mourning Dove

*Zenaida macroura*

Named for its mournful call, the Mourning Dove is the only North American dove found in every state and province from Alaska to Mexico. This fast-flying bird lives in small flocks, and begins to pair and nest long before most other species, sometimes even while winter snow lingers.

**HABITAT** *Visits backyards, fields, deserts, and also forests.*

pale blue ring around eye

wings uniformly brown above

gray-brown overall

black spots on back

long, pointed tail

buff colored belly

faint mottling on neck and underparts

**VOICE** *A hollow, sad, coah, cooo, cooo, coo.*
**NESTING** *Loose nest of sticks, usually in conifers; 2 eggs; 2 broods; February–October.*
**FEEDING** *Feeds almost exclusively on small seeds and grains. Eats cracked corn, millet, and sunflower seeds at feeders.*
**SIMILAR SPECIES** *Eurasian Collared-Dove, White-winged Dove.*

---

# Rock Pigeon

*Columba livia*

The wild ancestors of the feral Rock pigeon lived on Europe's sea cliffs. Today, tall buildings have replaced cliffs for the feral pigeon, a variable, colorful bird which frequents streets, parks, and other areas near people. Originally bred for racing and "homing", the Rock Pigeon usually mates for life.

**HABITAT** *Frequents city streets, parks, and barnyards.*

large white spot at base of bill

purple-green sheen to neck and breast

two black wing bars

dark bill

**ANCESTRAL FORM**

dark-tipped tail

compact body

reddish legs

**VOICE** *A low, cooing ooor-ooor or o-roo-coo.*
**NESTING** *Nest of twigs or grass, often on a balcony or ledge; 2 glossy white eggs; several broods; breeds year-round.*
**FEEDING** *Scavenges in cities; elsewhere eats seeds, leaves, buds, and invertebrates.*
**SIMILAR SPECIES** *Band-tailed Pigeon, Mourning Dove.*

**ANCESTRAL FORM**

variably colored body

**FERAL FORM**

# Anna's Hummingbird

*Calypte anna*

This is the most widespread hummingbird of the North American Pacific slope. It is an adaptable species, and often frequents human habitats. In courtship, males claim territory over a patch of flowers with a rich nectar supply. Females enter the male's territory, mate, and then leave to nest elsewhere.

**HABITAT** *Common in open woodlands, shrubby areas, backyards, and parks.*

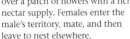

iridescent green upperparts

pale throat

♂

short, straight, bill

rose-red head, sides of neck, and throat

greenish sides and flanks

♂

slightly notched, dark green tail

green crown

mottled crown

♂♂

gray breast

♀

**VOICE** *Squeaking, grating calls; feeding call is chick.*
**NESTING** *Nest of plant down and spider webs, camouflaged by lichen; 1–3 pure white eggs; 2 broods; December–July.*
**FEEDING** *Tiny insects, spiders, and nectar.*
**SIMILAR SPECIES** *Costa's Hummingbird, Black-chinned Hummingbird.*

# Ruby-throated Hummingbird

*Archilochus colubris*

**HABITAT** *Open woods and gardens, where it sips nectar from flowers.*

Named for the male's dazzling throat, the Ruby-throated is the most common hummingbird in eastern North America. It performs a marathon fall migration, and its wings beat an incredible 80 times per second.

green crown

♂

glittering green upperparts

white chin and throat

♀

pale underparts

♂♀

bronzy green upperparts

orange-red throat

grayish white underparts

white chest

♂

dark, forked tail

greenish underparts

**VOICE** *Squeaky, high-pitched calls. Wings produce faint, high buzz.*
**NESTING** *Plant fiber and spiderweb nest; 2 white eggs; 1–2 broods; April–September.*
**FEEDING** *Eats tiny insects, spiders, and nectar, preferring red and orange flowers.*
**SIMILAR SPECIES** *Black-chinned Hummingbird, Broad-tailed Hummingbird.*

# Red-bellied Woodpecker

*Melanerpes carolinus*

**HABITAT** *Woods along rivers and swamps, and groves of mixed coniferous and deciduous trees.*

This species is named for the seldom-seen pale-red patch on the lower belly. It sometimes visits backyard feeders, but is most common in forests. It stores acorns, nuts, insects, and fruit for later meals, often hiding caches to safeguard against Pileated Woodpeckers.

red cap covers crown and nape

pale underparts

♂

regular black-and-white barring

barred upperparts

white patches at base of outer wing

gray crown

black upper tail feathers

♀

**VOICE** *Call is a loud, harsh, but rich kwirr, slightly rising. Also churr, chaw, and chiv, chiv.*
**NESTING** *Nesting cavity in partly decayed tree limb; 3–8 eggs; 1–3 broods; May–August.*
**FEEDING** *Drills into trees to extract beetle larvae; also eats berries and nuts.*
**SIMILAR SPECIES** *Golden-fronted Woodpecker, Gila Woodpecker.*

# Downy Woodpecker

*Picoides pubescans*

**HABITAT** *Forages at backyard feeders and in treetops.*

This is the smallest woodpecker in North America. Its size enables it to hang onto goldenrod stems, where it pecks the galls to extract fly larvae. Mated pairs stay together through the winter, and males often chase females from treetops, forcing them to feed lower in the tree.

white stripe above eye

very short bill

white underparts

♂

red nape patch

black wings with white spots

white back

black shoulders

♂

barred wings

black crown patch

spotted outermost tail feathers

white back

♀

**VOICE** *Call is a flat pick. Rapid whinny of calls descends in pitch.*
**NESTING** *Nest in tree cavity; 3–6 pure white eggs; 1 brood; May–July. Both parents incubate and feed the chicks.*
**FEEDING** *Excavates insect larvae from trees; readily consumes nuts and suet at feeders.*
**SIMILAR SPECIES** *Hairy Woodpecker.*

# Hairy Woodpecker

*Picoides villosus*

**HABITAT** *Woodlands and river groves, wherever large trees are present.*

The Hairy Woodpecker may occupy the same territory, with the same mate, for life. Both sexes defend territories with loud, fast drumming. Males strike tree trunks with their bills held sideways—the echoes help them detect the presence of beetle larvae. Females use their bills to seek insects under bark; each sex has a distinct food source.

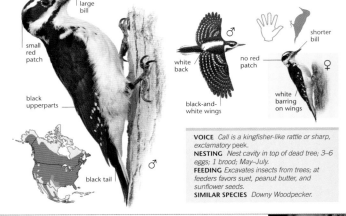

large bill

small red patch

black upperparts

black tail

white back

black-and-white wings

♂

no red patch

shorter bill

♀

white barring on wings

**VOICE** Call is a kingfisher-like rattle or sharp, exclamatory peek.
**NESTING** Nest cavity in top of dead tree; 3–6 eggs; 1 brood; May–July.
**FEEDING** Excavates insects from trees; at feeders favors suet, peanut butter, and sunflower seeds.
**SIMILAR SPECIES** Downy Woodpecker.

# Pileated Woodpecker

*Dryocopus pileatus*

This unmistakable crow-sized woodpecker occurs in every US state. Pairs require a large, forested territory, where they reside throughout the year, and excavate large, oblong nesting cavities. The Pileated Woodpecker occasionally visits feeders for suet to supplement its fall and winter fat reserves.

**HABITAT** *Forests; creates cavities in large, decaying trees.*

large black bill

red mustache

red crest

long neck

black back

white wing bar

white patch on wing

♂

long tail

♂

black mustache

♀

**VOICE** Loud irregular kik-kik-kikkik—kik-kik call. Males defend territory with persistent drumming and loud, trumpeting call.
**NESTING** Tree cavity nest; 3–5 white eggs; 1 brood; May–July.
**FEEDING** Termites, ants, and wood-boring beetle larvae. Acorns and fruit in winter.
**SIMILAR SPECIES** Ivory-billed Woodpecker.

# Eastern Phoebe

*Sayornis phoebe*

Among the first migrants to return in the spring, this bird is named for its raspy voice, which repeatedly says "phoebe." The Eastern Phoebe occasionally renovates previous nests or Barn Swallow nests. Its nests are often parasitized by Brown-headed Cowbirds, and may be abandoned if the cowbird lays its egg first.

**HABITAT** *Porches, eaves, rafters, and doorways. Also stream-bank cliffs and overhangs.*

white throat

large, dark head

gray-brown overall

long, dark tail

rounded wings with two faint wing bars

long, dark tail

dark eye

yellowish tint on lower belly

**VOICE** *Song is a burry, well-enunciated* fee-be *or* fi-bree. *Call is a sharp* chip.
**NESTING** *Substantial mud and grass nest covered with moss; 3–8 eggs; 2 broods; April–July. Female incubates; both feed chicks.*
**FEEDING** *Favors beetles, wasps, ants, and bees; also eats fish, frogs, berries, and seeds.*
**SIMILAR SPECIES** *Black Phoebe.*

# Steller's Jay

*Cyanocitta stelleri*

This bold bird was named for German naturalist Georg Steller, and is common at western campgrounds, parks, and backyards—wherever feeders and picnic items abound. It buries acorns as a winter food source. Steller's Jay varies in appearance across its range. It can imitate other birds, animals, and mechanical objects.

black crest

large, black head

**HABITAT** *Inhabits dense evergreen forests in western mountains.*

black-barred wings

long tail

long, straight bill

large, chunky body

rounded wings

dark blue body

**INTERIOR**

**INTERIOR**

**PACIFIC**

**VOICE** *Harsh scratchy* shook, shook.
**NESTING** *Bulky nest of stems, leaves, moss, and sticks with mud; 2–6 eggs; 1 brood; March–June.*
**FEEDING** *Eats insects, seeds, berries, nuts, small animals, eggs, and nestlings; also garbage, picnic, and feeder items.*
**SIMILAR SPECIES** *Blue Jay, Western Scrub Jay.*

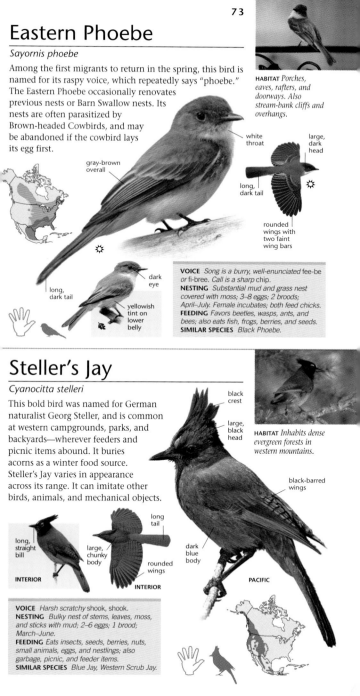

# Blue Jay

*Cyanocitta cristata*

This inquisitive, intelligent member of the crow family carries acorns far from the parent tree to bury them—nut-bearing trees may depend on jays for long-distance seed dispersal. Although the Blue Jay is known for its noisy, boisterous behavior, it generally becomes silent when nesting.

**HABITAT** *Favors suburbs, cities, and deciduous forests.*

crest

black patch between eye and bill

black necklace

blue back

bold white spots

broad, rounded wings

black legs

black barring on tail

**TIP**

*Attract Blue Jays by providing peanuts, cracked corn, and sunflower seeds on trays or in tube feeders with perches.*

**VOICE** *Harsh slurring jeeah or jay. Calls include musical queedle and pump.*
**NESTING** *Nest of sticks, moss, bark, lichen, and paper; 3–7 eggs; 1 brood; March–July.*
**FEEDING** *Prefers acorns, beech, and hickory nuts. Also eats corn, insects, fruits, and other birds' chicks and eggs.*
**SIMILAR SPECIES** *Steller's Jay.*

---

**HABITAT** *Frequents scrub oak forests; familiar western backyard resident.*

# Western Scrub Jay

*Aphelocoma californica*

The Western Scrub Jay caches seed, burying it for later retrieval. The seeds are buried whole, as they store better intact, and some later germinate—the Scrub Jay plays an important role in spreading forests. Backyard feeders may host several families of Scrub Jays at the same time.

white eyebrows

thick, black bill

rich blue neck and head

blue breast band

gray-blue or brownish back

**INTERIOR**

long, blue tail

**PACIFIC**

whitish underparts

dusky gray back

dull blue wings and tail

**INTERIOR**

**VOICE** *Call usually a harsh, rising shreeeeenk, may include low chudduk or clicking sounds.*
**NESTING** *Bulky stick nest close to the ground; 2–7 eggs; 1 brood; March–July.*
**FEEDING** *Eats mainly acorns and pine seeds; also insects, small birds, mice, and lizards; and sunflower seeds at feeders.*
**SIMILAR SPECIES** *Pinyon Jay.*

# American Crow

*Corvus brachynchos*

The American Crow is among the most intelligent of all birds. It works in groups to watch for danger, and offspring remain with their parents to help raise the broods of subsequent years. These offspring are useful helpers, participating in nest-building, incubating, and feeding new nestlings. Roosting flocks may contain as many as 200,000 birds.

**HABITAT** *Common in farmlands, cities, fields, and forests across North America.*

black overall, with greenish sheen

long, black bill

short tail

strong legs and feet

dull black overall

**VOICE** *A loud caw, cah, or kahr.*
**NESTING** *Bulky twig nest in tree fork; 3–9 gray-green, spotted eggs; 1 brood; April–June. Parents and siblings incubate and feed chicks.*
**FEEDING** *Feeds opportunistically on discarded grain, fruit, insects, eggs, chicks, small mammals, frogs, mollusks, and road kill.*
**SIMILAR SPECIES** *Northern Raven.*

# Purple Martin

*Progne subis*

The Purple Martin once nested in rock crevices and tree cavities. Now, nearly all martins nest in human-made structures, competing with many other bird species. This martin is a colonial nester, and inhabits huge fall roosts that include grackles and blackbirds.

**HABITAT** *Artificial nests and gourds, some rock crevices in western states.*

pale collar

♀

whitish gray underparts

♂

blue-black underparts

large, peaked head

long, forked black tail

blue-black upperparts

♂

long, dark, pointed wings

**VOICE** *Liquid warble; a throaty, rich tchew-wew, or pew, pew.*
**NESTING** *Nest of grass, twigs, and leaves; 3–8 pure white eggs; 1 brood; April–August.*
**FEEDING** *Forages in the air for a variety of flying insects.*
**SIMILAR SPECIES** *Tree Swallow, European Starling.*

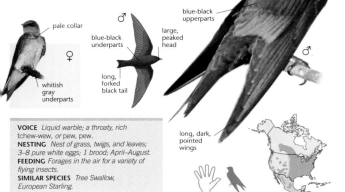

# Tufted Titmouse

*Baeolophus bicolor*

The Tufted Titmouse has recently expanded its range
farther north, perhaps due to the presence of garden bird
feeders. It is relatively tame, and has been known to take
sunflower seeds from people's
hands. When seeking hair for
its nest, the Tufted Titmouse
may pluck it from live
groundhogs, squirrels, and
opossums.

**HABITAT** *Urban areas, especially with large oak and beech trees.*

black forehead

crest

gray overall

short, broad tail

large black eye

whitish underparts

rust-colored flanks

**VOICE** *Low, clear whistle; also chants peter, peter, peter, or here, here, here, here.*
**NESTING** *Cavity nest of moss, bark, snake skin, and hair; 4–9 eggs; 1 brood; March–May.*
**FEEDING** *Favors acorns, beechnuts, insects, and fruit. Prefers sunflower seeds at feeders.*
**SIMILAR SPECIES** *Juniper Titmouse, Oak Titmouse.*

---

# Red-breasted Nuthatch

*Sitta canadensis*

The Red-breasted Nuthatch clings to branches and tree
trunks, where it hangs upside down to search for insects
and extract conifer seeds. At feeders, this feisty nuthatch is
capable of driving away larger birds. It often caches seeds
in tree crevices, sometimes using lichen or bark
for camouflage.

**HABITAT** *Northern coniferous forests, and nest boxes.*

rounded wings

♂

long, pointed beak

slightly muted head pattern

stubby, square-cut tail

white line above eye

♀

bluish back

broad black line over eye

rust colored underparts ♂

**VOICE** *High, nasal ank or enk.*
**NESTING** *Nesting cavity in dead tree, abandoned woodpecker cavities, and nest boxes. 4–7 eggs; 1 brood; May–July. Female incubates, both parents feed chicks.*
**FEEDING** *Eats mainly conifer seeds; at feeders favors sunflower seeds, nuts, and suet.*
**SIMILAR SPECIES** *White-Breasted Nuthatch.*

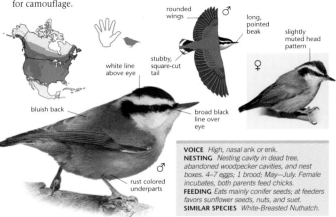

# White-breasted Nuthatch

*Sitta caroliensis*

The White-breasted Nuthatch moves head-first down tree trunks in search of insects. It favors hulled sunflower seeds from feeders, which it caches, and then consumes at night before roosting. In contrast, sunflower seeds with shells are eaten during the day, when there is enough light by which to extract the kernels. Females cache seeds farther from feeders, as males steal their food. In winter, this nuthatch joins chickadee flocks, sometimes stealing cached food from flock members. The nuthatch lets the chickadee watch for predators, and recognizes its warning calls.

**HABITAT** *Deciduous forests and trees across the US.*

rounded wings

white flashes on tail

♂

white face

black eye

black crown

blue-gray upperparts

slightly upturned bill

whitish gray underparts

♂

short, broad tail

chestnut undertail

gray crown

dull gray upperparts

whitish underparts

♀

**TIP**

*To encourage White-breasted Nuthatches to frequent your property, stock feeders with suet, hulled peanuts, peanut butter, and both hulled and unhulled sunflower seeds. Since nuthatches nest in tree cavities, mount nest boxes on trees, or use a drill to create cavity starts for them in dead forest trees.*

**VOICE** *Excited nasal yank-yank-yank call.*
**NESTING** *Nest in abandoned woodpecker cavities or knotholes that lead to rotten tree interiors; 5–8 heavily spotted eggs; 1 brood; April–June. Female incubates; both parents feed chicks.*
**FEEDING** *Favors acorns, beechnuts, and insects and beetles picked from the bark of tree trunks; all types of sunflower seeds from feeders.*
**SIMILAR SPECIES** *Red-breasted Nuthatch.*

# Black-capped Chickadee

*Poecile atricapillus*

The tiny Black-capped Chickadee survives cold northern winters by frenetically gathering food, consuming as many calories by day as it loses at night, and hiding hundreds of seeds daily. Winter flocks huddle together in tree cavities, dropping body temperatures to conserve energy and fluffing feathers for insulation.

**HABITAT** *Thrives in extreme northern habitats.*

large white cheek patch

black cap and bib

white on wings and tail

white edges on wing feathers

short black bill

white edges on outer tail feathers

relatively long tail

faded buff flanks

grayish brown upperparts

**VOICE** *Song a clear whistle, fe-bee-ee or fee-bee, with the first note higher. Also a clear chick-a-dee-dee-dee, or dee-dee-dee.*
**NESTING** *Nest in tree cavity; 5–10 eggs; 1 brood; April–June.*
**FEEDING** *Eats insects, seeds, and berries. At feeders, favors sunflower seeds and suet.*
**SIMILAR SPECIES** *Carolina Chickadee.*

**TIP**
*To attract chickadees, mount nest boxes, drill cavities in dead trees, and offer sunflower seeds and suet at feeders.*

---

# House Wren

*Troglodytes aedon*

Named for its association with humans, the feisty House Wren is a gardener's best friend, feeding almost entirely on insects. The male starts multiple nests, often in peculiar locations such as watering cans and flowerpots. The female then chooses a male and selects one of his nests, adding a soft lining.

**HABITAT** *Frequents shrubby backyards and forest edges.*

drab brown plumage

light eye ring

gray-brown body

slightly downturned bill

pale underparts

**WESTERN**

**EASTERN**

pale brown crown

**EASTERN**

**VOICE** *Song a series of rattles ending with descending liquid trills. Low, dry, raspy call.*
**NESTING** *Stick nest in box or other cavity; 5–12 white eggs; 2–3 broods; April–July.*
**FEEDING** *Eats grasshoppers, caterpillars, ants, bees, wasps, flies, and ticks.*
**SIMILAR SPECIES** *Winter Wren, Bewick's Wren.*

# Cedar Waxwing

*Bombycilla cedorum*

This sociable bird is named for its waxy red wing-feather tips and consumption of cedar fruits. The red wax on its wing tips indicates age, and may play a role in mate choice, as older pairs breed more successfully.

**HABITAT** *Open woods and orchards; wherever fruiting trees abound.*

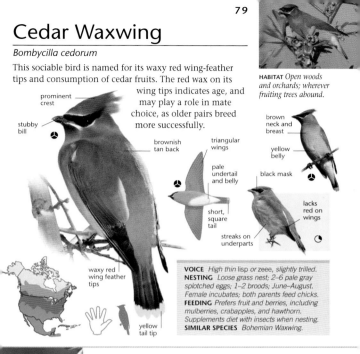

prominent crest

stubby bill

brownish tan back

triangular wings

pale undertail and belly

short, square tail

streaks on underparts

brown neck and breast

yellow belly

black mask

lacks red on wings

waxy red wing feather tips

yellow tail tip

**VOICE** *High thin lisp or zeee, slightly trilled.*
**NESTING** *Loose grass nest; 2–6 pale gray splotched eggs; 1–2 broods; June–August. Female incubates; both parents feed chicks.*
**FEEDING** *Prefers fruit and berries, including mulberries, crabapples, and hawthorn. Supplements diet with insects when nesting.*
**SIMILAR SPECIES** *Bohemian Waxwing.*

# Mountain Bluebird

*Sialia curucoides*

**HABITAT** *Frequents western mountain meadows and foothills, often near aspens, cottonwoods, and ranches.*

The Mountain Bluebird perches or hovers near the ground, dropping to capture prey. It also catches flying insects on the wing. Populations have declined due to the introduction of the House Sparrow and the European Starling, which compete for nesting cavities.

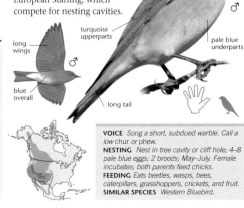

turquoise upperparts

pale blue underparts

♂

lightly spotted back

blue wings and tail

long wings

blue overall

♂

long tail

gray-brown head and body ♀

whitish belly

**VOICE** *Song a short, subdued warble. Call a low chur or phew.*
**NESTING** *Nest in tree cavity or cliff hole; 4–8 pale blue eggs; 2 broods; May–July. Female incubates; both parents feed chicks.*
**FEEDING** *Eats beetles, wasps, bees, caterpillars, grasshoppers, crickets, and fruit.*
**SIMILAR SPECIES** *Western Bluebird.*

# Eastern Bluebird

*Sialia sialis*

The Eastern Bluebird has wide appeal because of its glorious color, cheerful song, and readiness to use birdhouses. Artificial housing is important for the species, as natural tree cavities are often occupied by House Sparrows and European Starlings. A bluebird can spot insect prey from up to 50 yards away.

**HABITAT** *Forest clearings, farms, open country with scattered trees.*

stout bill

rufous breast and throat

short wings

♂

bluish gray underwings

rusty underparts

bright blue upperparts

♂

white belly

white undertail

blue-gray back

♀

light orange underparts

☾

gray-brown upperparts

spotted throat and breast

**VOICE** *Song a short series of soft, musical notes. Call a musical* chur-wi *or* tru-ly.
**NESTING** *Nests in birdhouses, tree cavities; 2–7 eggs; 2 broods, February–September. Female incubates; both feed the chicks.*
**FEEDING** *Eats insects including crickets, grasshoppers, and caterpillars.*
**SIMILAR SPECIES** *Western Bluebird.*

# American Robin

*Turdus migratorius*

The American Robin abandons northern latitudes in favor of southeastern states each fall. It is territorial when nesting, even chasing its own reflection, but may live in flocks of thousands in the winter. Dried fruit is important in early spring, when snow prevents the robin from catching earthworms.

**HABITAT** *Parks, streets, and suburbs. Needs mature trees for nesting and singing.*

broken white eye ring

blackish head and nape

dark gray back

♂

blackish tail

brick red breast

♂

dark head

complete white eye ring

gray back

♀

orangey red breast

mottled gray back

☾

spotted breast

**VOICE** *Song a clear caroling with short phrases. Calls are* tyeep *and* tut-tut-tut.
**NESTING** *Nest in protected conifers, building gutters, or eaves; 3–7 blue eggs; 2–3 broods; April–July. Female incubates; both feed young.*
**FEEDING** *Berries from trees and shrubs; earthworms in the warmer months.*
**SIMILAR SPECIES** *Varied Thrush.*

# Northern Mockingbird

*Mimus polyglottos*

The Northern Mockingbird is resident throughout the US, and has begun expanding northward. Its repertoire of songs is estimated to include imitations of over 50 bird species. The diversity of its song reflects the age and experience of the male singer, and females choose mates accordingly.

**HABITAT** *Favors thickets and suburban environments.*

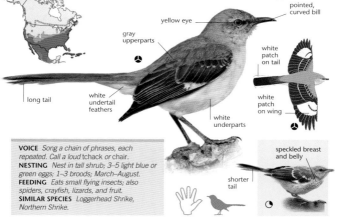

pointed, curved bill

yellow eye

gray upperparts

white patch on tail

white patch on wing

long tail

white undertail feathers

white underparts

shorter tail

speckled breast and belly

**VOICE** *Song a chain of phrases, each repeated. Call a loud tchack or chair.*
**NESTING** *Nest in tall shrub; 3–5 light blue or green eggs; 1–3 broods; March–August.*
**FEEDING** *Eats small flying insects; also spiders, crayfish, lizards, and fruit.*
**SIMILAR SPECIES** *Loggerhead Shrike, Northern Shrike.*

# European Starling

*Sturnus vulgaris*

The European Starling is given its name by the star-spangled look that emerges after its late summer molt. It is a sociable and adaptable bird that competes with native birds for tree cavities, and descends on feeders and cultivated fruit in large numbers.

**HABITAT** *Found across the US, wherever there are trees.*

yellow bill

triangular wings

short, squared-off tail

black bill

wing feathers have orange edges

**NONBREEDING**

dull brownish head

glossy dark plumage with a colorful sheen

**BREEDING**

**BREEDING**

reddish brown legs

dark bill

plain brown body

**VOICE** *Song a medley of rattles, squeaks, and whistles, with mimicked calls of other species.*
**NESTING** *Cavity in tree or building crevice; 4–7 blue-green eggs; 1–2 broods; March–July.*
**FEEDING** *Eats earthworms, ants, bees, wasps, spiders, fruit, and suet.*
**SIMILAR SPECIES** *Red-winged Blackbird, Purple Martin.*

# Northern Cardinal

*Cardinalis cardinalis*

No fewer than seven eastern states claim the Northern Cardinal as their state bird. Despite this popularity, its vibrant color, and its exuberant singing, this bird has a shy demeanor around bird feeders, often approaching at dusk and dawn. Its large beak permits the consumption of a wide range of wild fruits and weed seeds. Bird feeders and warmer winters have contributed to its northward expansion, and these cardinals are widespread and abundant. The Northern Cardinal resides year-round in southern states, and often does so in the north as well.

**HABITAT** *Brushy habitats including woodland edges, thickets, and gardens.*

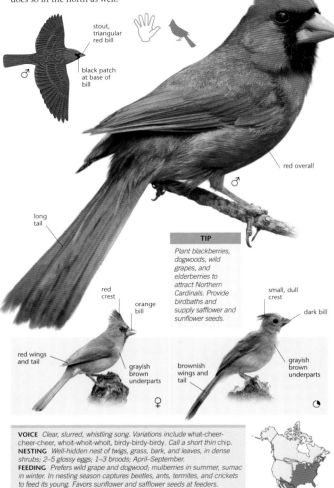

stout, triangular red bill

black patch at base of bill

♂

distinct crest

red overall

♂

long tail

red crest

orange bill

red wings and tail

grayish brown underparts

♀

small, dull crest

dark bill

brownish wings and tail

grayish brown underparts

☽

**TIP**

*Plant blackberries, dogwoods, wild grapes, and elderberries to attract Northern Cardinals. Provide birdbaths and supply safflower and sunflower seeds.*

**VOICE** Clear, slurred, whistling song. Variations include what-cheer-cheer-cheer, whoit-whoit-whoit, birdy-birdy-birdy. Call a short thin chip.
**NESTING** Well-hidden nest of twigs, grass, bark, and leaves, in dense shrubs; 2–5 glossy eggs; 1–3 broods; April–September.
**FEEDING** Prefers wild grape and dogwood; mulberries in summer, sumac in winter. In nesting season captures beetles, ants, termites, and crickets to feed its young. Favors sunflower and safflower seeds at feeders.
**SIMILAR SPECIES** Pyrrhuloxia.

# Rose-breasted Grosbeak

*Pheucticus ludovicianus*

The dazzling rose-colored breast for which it is named makes the male Rose-breasted Grosbeak an easily recognized sign of spring. The male returns first after migration to establish its territory. Males compete for a female's attention by hovering and singing.

**HABITAT** *Forests, gardens, and parks with mature deciduous trees.*

large, thick, pale bill

large, rose-red triangle on breast

white belly

white flashes on black plumage

♂ **BREEDING**

short tail with white corners

♂ **BREEDING**

streaked plumage

♂ **NONBREEDING**

rosy or orange breast

☽ ♂ **1ST**

white marks

brown streaked plumage

♀

**VOICE** Loud, robin-like, caroling song with run-on phrases. Call a metallic kick or eek.
**NESTING** Nests in thickets; 3–5 pale gray or blue-green eggs; 1–2 broods; May–July. Both parents incubate and feed chicks.
**FEEDING** Eats beetles, caterpillars, fruit, seeds, and buds. Sunflower seeds at feeders.
**SIMILAR SPECIES** Black-headed Grosbeak.

---

# American Tree Sparrow

*Spizella arborea*

Given ample food, this hardy sparrow can withstand temperatures as low as 18°F (–8°C). Typically a ground feeder, it is able to cling to wind-tossed plant stems while eating seeds. The female typically lines the nest with soft ptarmigan feathers and lemming fur.

**HABITAT** *Fields and shrublands across most of the US.*

rusty cap

dark spot on gray breast

two white wing bars

🟢 **BREEDING**

bill dark above, yellow below

long, squarish tail

gray head and nape

🟢 **BREEDING**

**VOICE** Song sweet and variable, opening with one or two high clear notes. Call is tseet.
**NESTING** Cup-shaped grassy nest; 3-7 pale blue speckled eggs; 1 brood; June–July.
**FEEDING** Prefers weed seeds, including grass, ragweed, and lamb's quarters.
**SIMILAR SPECIES** Chipping Sparrow, Field Sparrow.

rusty tones on shoulders and wings

🟢

striped back

cleft tail

🟢 **NONBREEDING**

# Chipping Sparrow

*Spizella pusilla*

The Chipping Sparrow has readily adapted to human habitats—especially parks and suburban areas, where it frequents tall trees, shrubs, and lawns. Over a single winter, each bird consumes about 2¼ pounds of weed seeds—160 times its body weight.

**HABITAT** *Gardens, orchards, forest clearings, and farmyards.*

rusty cap

white stripe above eye

black eye stripe

streaked upperparts

pale underwings

blackish bill

gray breast

relatively short, notched tail

pinkish bill

rusty crown

heavily streaked plumage

**VOICE** *Song a long simple trill. Call a sharp chip.*
**NESTING** *Grassy, cup-shaped nest, often lined with horsehair, on conifer branch; 2–5 eggs; 1–2 broods; April–August.*
**FEEDING** *Eats ragweed, amaranth, and crabgrass seeds. Feeds insects to young.*
**SIMILAR SPECIES** *Tree Sparrow, Field Sparrow.*

# Song Sparrow

*Melospiza melodia*

The Song Sparrow varies regionally in size, color, and migratory habits—northern birds migrate, most others do not. In cold weather, each bird must eat between 85 and 4,000 seeds per hour to survive, depending on the size of the seeds.

**HABITAT** *Brushy fencerows and fields throughout North America.*

heavily streaked upperparts

stout bill

rounded head

broad, rounded wings

paler neck

more rusty overall

whitish lower belly

heavily streaked breast

**WEST COAST**

**SOUTHWEST**

**WEST COAST**

grayish brown head

**EASTERN**

**VOICE** *Song begins with bright, repetitive notes:* sweet sweet sweet. *Call low, nasal* tchep.
**NESTING** *First nest in grass clumps; later nests in shrubs; 3–5 greenish, blotched eggs; 1–3 broods; March–August.*
**FEEDING** *Eats mostly seeds, but in summer insects and fruit constitute half its diet.*
**SIMILAR SPECIES** *Fox Sparrow.*

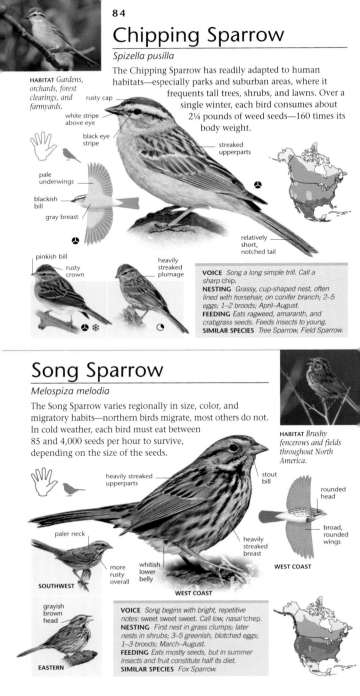

# Dark-eyed Junco

*Junco hyemalis*

The Dark-eyed Junco visits more North American feeders than any other bird species. But even when feeders are well-stocked with millet and cracked corn, it still feeds primarily on weed seeds, consuming thousands every day.

**HABITAT** *Northern coniferous forests; winters near open woods, yards.*

small, pinkish bill

dark gray body

white belly

♂ **SLATE-COLORED**

dull brownish back

bluish gray hood

♀ **PINK-SIDED**

reddish brown back

black mask

pale gray underparts

♂ **GRAY-HEADED**

rusty colored back

♂ **OREGON**

blackish hood

white outer tail feathers

♂ **SLATE-COLORED**

**VOICE** *Song a loose musical trill. Call a light smack or tick.*
**NESTING** *Usually nests on ground or in low shrub, hidden by overhead foliage; 3–6 eggs; 1–2 broods; May–August.*
**FEEDING** *Prefers seeds. Also eats insects, and feeds them to its chicks.*
**SIMILAR SPECIES** *Yellow-eyed Junco.*

# Red-winged Blackbird

*Agelaius phoeniceus*

The Red-winged Blackbird is abundant, due to its ability to glean leftover grain from agricultural fields and feedlots. In winter, it forms huge roosts with other blackbirds. Males are bold nest defenders, chasing away much larger birds.

**HABITAT** *Prefers marshy habitats; also wet meadows, fields, and pastures.*

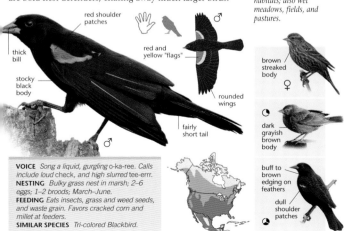

red shoulder patches

thick bill

stocky black body

♂

red and yellow "flags"

rounded wings

fairly short tail

♂

brown streaked body

♀

dark grayish brown body

buff to brown edging on feathers

dull shoulder patches

**VOICE** *Song a liquid, gurgling o-ka-ree. Calls include loud check, and high slurred tee-errr.*
**NESTING** *Bulky grass nest in marsh; 2–6 eggs; 1–2 broods; March–June.*
**FEEDING** *Eats insects, grass and weed seeds, and waste grain. Favors cracked corn and millet at feeders.*
**SIMILAR SPECIES** *Tri-colored Blackbird.*

# Common Grackle

*Quiscalus quiscala*

This feisty blackbird appears black at a distance, but close up its iridescent plumage is sensational. Grackles exploit food as opportunity permits—some even take the eggs and young of other birds. The Common Grackle sometimes feeds near freshwater streams and ponds.

**HABITAT** *Backyards, parks, and deciduous forests.*

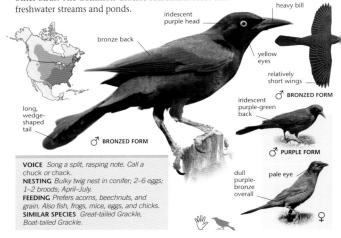

iridescent purple head

heavy bill

bronze back

yellow eyes

relatively short wings

♂ **BRONZED FORM**

iridescent purple-green back

♂ **PURPLE FORM**

long, wedge-shaped tail

♂ **BRONZED FORM**

dull purple-bronze overall

pale eye

♀

**VOICE** *Song a split, rasping note. Call a chuck or chack.*
**NESTING** *Bulky twig nest in conifer; 2–6 eggs; 1–2 broods; April–July.*
**FEEDING** *Prefers acorns, beechnuts, and grain. Also fish, frogs, mice, eggs, and chicks.*
**SIMILAR SPECIES** *Great-tailed Grackle, Boat-tailed Grackle.*

---

# Bullock's Oriole

*Icterus bullockii*

The Bullock's Oriole was once considered to be part of the same species as the Baltimore Oriole. The two species interbreed where their ranges overlap on the western Great Plains. The song of the female Bullock's Oriole ends with harsher notes than that of the male.

**HABITAT** *Common in open western woodlands; prefers tall streamside trees.*

black throat

black back and wings

bold white shoulder patch

orange-yellow underparts

♂

♂

gray legs and toes

bright yellow head

gray back and wings

♂ **1ST**

pale yellow underparts

♀

olive tail

**VOICE** *Song a series of whistled notes interspersed with rattles. Chattering call.*
**NESTING** *Hanging nest woven from horsehair and plants; 2–7 eggs; 1 brood; March–June.*
**FEEDING** *Eats berries, nectar, and insects. At feeders consumes sugar water and fruit.*
**SIMILAR SPECIES** *Baltimore Oriole, Hooded Oriole.*

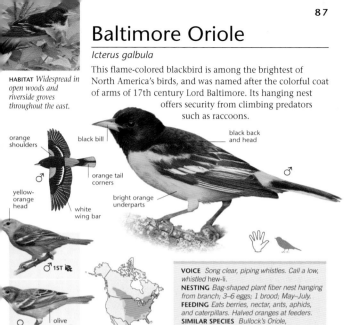

# Baltimore Oriole

*Icterus galbula*

**HABITAT** *Widespread in open woods and riverside groves throughout the east.*

This flame-colored blackbird is among the brightest of North America's birds, and was named after the colorful coat of arms of 17th century Lord Baltimore. Its hanging nest offers security from climbing predators such as raccoons.

orange shoulders

black bill

black back and head

♂

orange tail corners

yellow-orange head

bright orange underparts

white wing bar

♂

♂ 1ST

olive overall

♀

**VOICE** *Song clear, piping whistles. Call a low, whistled hew-li.*
**NESTING** *Bag-shaped plant fiber nest hanging from branch; 3–6 eggs; 1 brood; May–July.*
**FEEDING** *Eats berries, nectar, ants, aphids, and caterpillars. Halved oranges at feeders.*
**SIMILAR SPECIES** *Bullock's Oriole, American Redstart.*

# Purple Finch

*Carpodacuss purpureus*

**HABITAT** *Northeastern coniferous forests. Winters in backyards, fields, and shrubland.*

More raspberry than purple, this colorful finch has declined throughout the east due to habitat loss and competition from introduced birds. When courting, a male vibrates his wings into a blur, hovers above a prospective mate, and sings softly to her.

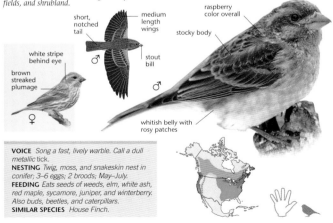

raspberry color overall

short, notched tail

medium length wings

stocky body

♂

stout bill

white stripe behind eye

♂

brown streaked plumage

♀

whitish belly with rosy patches

**VOICE** *Song a fast, lively warble. Call a dull metallic tick.*
**NESTING** *Twig, moss, and snakeskin nest in conifer; 3–6 eggs; 2 broods; May–July.*
**FEEDING** *Eats seeds of weeds, elm, white ash, red maple, sycamore, juniper, and winterberry. Also buds, beetles, and caterpillars.*
**SIMILAR SPECIES** *House Finch.*

# House Finch

*Carpodacus mexicanus*

The population of wild eastern House Finches was established in 1940, when pet store owners on Long Island, New York, released their illegal stocks to avoid prosecution. The color of individual males reflects the diversity of their diet and, when given a choice, females usually select more colorful males.

**HABITAT** *Wild parts of the West, settled areas across the US.*

red bib and head

short, rounded wings

red face

long, notched tail

brown upperparts

streaked belly

♂ **BREEDING**

dull grayish streaks

♀

long tail feathers

♂ **BREEDING**

pinkish head

♂ **NONBREEDING**

**VOICE** *Bright song is loose and disjointed, ending in a harsh nasal where or che-urrr.*
**NESTING** *Grassy nest, often behind gutters, porch lights, and other building crevices; 2–6 eggs; 2–3 broods; March–August.*
**FEEDING** *Favors thistle, dandelion, and other seeds. Prefers sunflower seeds at feeders.*
**SIMILAR SPECIES** *Purple Finch.*

---

# House Sparrow

*Passer domesticus*

Native to Europe, the House Sparrow was introduced to New York City around 1851. Its successful competition with native birds for nesting cavities, and adaptability to local foods—including gleaning meals from dumpsters—has made it one of the most abundant North American birds.

**HABITAT** *Thrives in areas close to humans, who inadvertently provide housing and food.*

black throat and bib

chestnut nape

black-and-brown streaks on upperparts

stout black bill

gray breast

short wings

♂ ☀

♂ ☀

short tail

buff eyestripe

♀

yellowish bill

beige overall

**VOICE** *Song a monotonous series of chirps. Call a husky fillip.*
**NESTING** *Bulky grass and debris nest in house or barn crevice; 4–6 greenish white, dark-spotted eggs; 2–3 broods; April–August.*
**FEEDING** *Forages on ground, gleaning sidewalk crumbs and spilled grain.*
**SIMILAR SPECIES** *Indigo Bunting.*

# American Goldfinch

*Carduelis tristis*

In warmer months it's hard to miss the lemon-yellow American Goldfinch, but in winter, when it turns olive, this bird is often overlooked or misidentified. This goldfinch is often resident throughout the year, and a variety of adaptations help it survive cold weather. It fills its bill late each day to provide a seed supply for the night, and chooses protected shelters for roosting. Goldfinches defer nesting until late summer, waiting until their favorite seeds are abundant. During courtship and incubation, the female relies on the male to feed her, sometimes begging like a nestling when he arrives with food.

**HABITAT** *Meadows, roadsides, gardens, and open woods with thistle and weed patches.*

black forehead and crown

white wing bar

black tail

bright yellow underparts

♂ **BREEDING**

yellow throat and collar

tan back

pale tan underparts

♂ **NONBREEDING**

olive colored overall

dull yellow throat

♀ **NONBREEDING**

pinkish bill

bright yellow back

white wing bar

♂ **NONBREEDING**

brownish olive back

yellow underparts

♀ **BREEDING**

---

**TIP**

*Attract American Goldfinches to your garden by planting birches, elms, maples, alders, sunflowers, cosmos, and coneflowers. These birds will come to all types of feeders, and will even eat the seeds that fall to the ground beneath a feeder. Stock backyard feeders with nyger and black oil sunflower seeds.*

---

**VOICE** Song is clear, sustained, canary-like. In flight, repeats ti-dee-di-di, or potato-chip.
**NESTING** Compact, woven plant fiber nest with thistle down lining, located in dense shrubs; 4–6 pale bluish, unmarked eggs; 1–2 broods; July–September. Female incubates; both parents feed chicks.
**FEEDING** Seeds from conifers, thistle, goldenrods, asters, and burdock. In gardens, eats coneflower, coreopsis, cosmos, and lettuce seeds.
**SIMILAR SPECIES** Evening Grosbeak.

# The Great Backyard Bird Count

**Now that you've become fascinated by birds and started to attract them to your backyard, you'll want to ensure that they brighten the backyards of future generations. One of the best ways to do this is to join Audubon, and participate in programs such as the Great Backyard Bird Count and eBird.**

Tens of thousands of bird watchers of all ages and levels of experience take part in the Great Backyard Bird Count (GBBC) for four days each February. These citizen scientists create a real-time snapshot of where birds are across the continent, and learn more about the birds in their regions. In 2009, over 93,000 checklists were submitted. Co-sponsored by the National Audubon Society and the Cornell Lab of Ornithology, the count began in 1998, with the goal of engaging everyday citizens in counting and appreciating birds. Since then, more and more people have taken part each year. The GBBC is a great way to learn more about the birds in your backyard. It is also a fun, engaging, and educational activity for families and groups, including schools, and an ideal way for more accomplished birders to introduce others to the wonderful world of birds.

## How to take part

To take part in the Great Backyard Bird Count, you need to observe and count birds for at least 15 minutes at a time, on one or more days of the count, and keep a note of the birds that you see on a checklist. Submit a separate checklist for each new day that you count—you can submit

**Anna's Hummingbird**
*This beautiful hummingbird could be the highlight of a 15 minute count.*

**11,550,200 birds from 619 species were counted in 2009.**

**Feeding frenzy**
*House Finches flock to this feeder, which is designed to deter squirrels while providing for birds at multiple levels.*

more than one checklist per day if you count birds in multiple locations that day. Tally and keep note of the greatest number of individuals of each species that you see together at any one time. You may find it helpful to print a regional bird checklist from www.birdcount. org to get an idea of the birds you're likely to see. When you're finished, enter your results on the website—you'll see a button marked "Enter Your Checklists!" which will be there from the first day of the count until the deadline for submission, typically the first day of March.

## What we learn

Whether you count four species at your backyard birdfeeder or 75 species in a day's visit to a wildlife refuge, you contribute valuable information for science and conservation. Each year the GBBC provides a real-time snapshot of bird distribution across North America. It shows how birds are responding to changes in weather patterns, available food sources, and other environmental conditions. With all of the results publicly available online, anyone can explore the data to see how birds are faring in their area. As the count grows, participants help add new species to the count. For example, in 2009 we added two oceanic species for the first time, obtained first-time reports of lingering migratory species, and added two rare Mexican species. There are many ways for volunteers

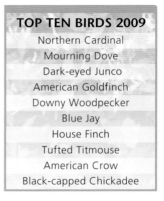

### TOP TEN BIRDS 2009
Northern Cardinal
Mourning Dove
Dark-eyed Junco
American Goldfinch
Downy Woodpecker
Blue Jay
House Finch
Tufted Titmouse
American Crow
Black-capped Chickadee

to help GBBC grow. Visit www.birdcount.org to learn how you can help make the GBBC an even bigger success.

## eBird

A real-time, online checklist program, eBird has revolutionized the way the birding community reports information. Launched in 2002 by the Cornell Lab of Ornithology and Audubon, eBird provides rich data sources for basic information on bird abundance and distribution. Over 10 million records are submitted to eBird each year. eBird's goal is to maximize the usefulness of these observations by sharing them with educators, land managers, ornithologists, and conservation biologists. eBird provides tools in English, French, and Spanish that help birders maintain their records and enable them to visualize data with interactive maps, graphs, and bar charts. A birder simply enters when, where, and how he or she went birding, then fills out a checklist of the birds seen and heard during the outing. To participate, visit www.ebird.org.

## About Audubon

The Audubon mission is to conserve and restore natural ecosystems, focusing on birds, other wildlife, and their habitats, for the benefit of

**Eastern Phoebe**
*The Eastern Phoebe often nests near people on porch eves or in trees, making it easy to spot.*

**Northern Cardinal**
*Northern cardinals are flashy year-round residents, that are spreading their range to Canada.*

and restoring critical wildlife habitat to implementing healthy habitat practices in their own backyards. Audubon's public policy programs are supported by a strong foundation of science, environmental education, and grassroots engagement. Working with a network of state offices, chapters, and volunteers, Audubon works to protect and restore our natural heritage.

To learn how you can support **Audubon**, call **(212) 979-3000**, visit **www.audubon.org**, or write to **Audubon, 225 Varick Street, New York, New York 10014.**

humanity and the Earth's biological diversity.

Through education, science, and public policy initiatives, Audubon engages people throughout the US and Latin America in conservation. Audubon's Centers, and its sanctuaries and education programs, are developing the next generation of conservation leaders by providing opportunities for people to learn about and enjoy the natural world. The science program is focused on connecting people with nature through projects like Audubon at Home and the Christmas Bird Count. Audubon's volunteer Citizen Scientists participate in research and conservation action in a variety of ways, from monitoring bird populations

**Watching birds**
*Birding is becoming a national pastime: only binoculars and a field guide are required.*

# Index

Page numbers in **bold**
refer to bird profiles.

# Acknowledgments

DK Publishing would like to thank Sandra Pinto of Audubon for her many helpful suggestions on the text and Colin Hynson for indexing.

The publisher would like to thank the following for their kind permission to reproduce their photographs:

**(Key: a-above; b-below/bottom; c-center; l-left; r-right; t-top)**

1 FLPA: S & D & K Maslowski. 2 Cal Vornberger: (b). 3 Corbis: William Manning (tr). Dudley Edmondson: (cra). Getty: Stephen J. Krasemann (crb). Getty: Daniel J. Cox (br). 4 FLPA: S & D & K Maslowski. 5 Cal Vornberger: (cra). 6 Dudley Edmondson: (bl). Peter S Weber: (br). 7 RSPB: (cla). 8-9 Cal Vornberger. 10 Joe Fuhrman: (bl). 11 Joe Fuhrman: (br). Cal Vornberger: (t). 12 Cal Vornberger: (b). 13 Andy & Gill Swash: (tr). Cal Vornberger: (cl) (br). 14 Jari Peltomäki: (bl). 15 Cal Vornberger: (b). 16-17 Cal Vornberger: (b). 17 Western Foundation of Vertebrate Zoology (WFVZ) : (cl). 19 Cal Vornberger: (tl). 20 rspb-images. com: Richard Brooks (tr). Cal Vornberger: (bl). 21 rspb-images.com: Tony Hamblin (b). 22 Cal Vornberger: (tr) (b). 23 Cal Vornberger: (tr). 24 Dudley Edmondson: (bl). Cal Vornberger: (bc) (br). 25 Cal Vornberger. 26 Cal Vornberger: (bl) (br). 27 Brian Small. 28 Garth McElroy: (bl). Cal Vornberger: (br). 29 EJ Peiker. 30 Jari Peltomäki: (bc) (br). Markus Varesvuo: (bl). 31 Cal Vornberger. 32-33 Photolibrary: Richard Day. 36 Dudley Edmondson: (bl). 37 Corbis: Robert Landau: (br). 38 Flickr.com: Glenn Seplak (br). 39 Cal Vornberger: (t). 40 Dudley Edmondson: (bl). RSPB: (cr). 41 Dudley Edmondson: (br). Peter S Weber: (t). 42 FLPA: S & D & K Maslowski (t). Getty Images: Joel Sartore (b). 43 Corbis: George McCarthy (t). 44 iStockphoto.com: Marcel Pelletier (b). 46 Cal Vornberger: (b). 47 Brian Small: (t). 48 Cal Vornberger: (bl). 49 Cal Vornberger. 50 Corbis: Lynda Richardson: (t). Cal Vornberger: (b). 51 FLPA: David Hosking (t). 52 Corbis: Lynda Richardson (r). Getty Images: Jack Zehrt (l). 54-55 rspb-images.com: Geoff Dore. 56 Markus Varesvuo. 57 Dudley Edmondson: (br). 58 Cal Vornberger: (b). 59 DK Images: Kim Taylor (t). Flickr.com: Kevin J. O'Connor (c). Geocities.com: (cr). Tomi Muukonen: (br). 60 Peter S Weber: (b). 61 Joe Fuhrman: (b). Cal Vornberger: (cla). Peter S Weber: (cl). 63 Jari Peltomäki: (t). Markus Varesvuo: (crb). 64 Peter S Weber: (b). 65 Dudley Edmondson: (cl). Joe Fuhrman: (tl). Brian Small: (cr). 66-67 Cal Vornberger: (tr). 69 Corbis: Gary W. Carter (tl). 70 Corbis: Richard Hamilton Smith (clb). 71 Corbis: Gary W. Carter (tl). 72 Getty: Joel Sartore (tl). Corbis: Joel W. Rogers (crb). 73 Alamy: Rolf Nussbaumer (tr). Corbis: Perry Conway (crb). 75 Steve Kress (clb). 77 Corbis: Gary W. Carter (tr). 78 Getty: Michael S. Quinton (tl). Corbis: Visuals Unlimited (clb). 79 Getty: Charles Melto (tr). 80 Getty: Steve Maslowski (tl). Getty: Klaus Nigge (clb). 81 Getty: Steve Maslowski (tl). 82 Carol Polich (tr). 83 Getty; altrendonature (tr). Getty: Steve Maslowski (crb). 84 Alamy: Rick and Nora Bowers: (tl). Getty: Joel Sartore (crb). 85 Corbis: Gary W. Carter (tl). 86 Corbis: Gary W. Carter (tr). Getty: Jeremy Woodhouse (clb). 88 Getty: Charles Melton (tr). 89 Corbis: Lynda Richardson (tr). 90 Getty: Judy Wantulok. 91 Getty: Bates Littlehales. 93 Getty: Macduff Everton (br).

All other images © Dorling Kindersley
For further information see:
**www.dkimages.com**